CONTENTS

KW-057-110

PREFACE

My involvement with animal feeds and livestock nutrition during the past 20 years has led me to believe that a concise but comprehensive reference book summarising the main physical and nutritional characteristics of the raw materials available as livestock feeds in the UK would be welcomed by many.

Classic works such as those of Morrison, Schneider and Bo Göhl are not readily available, are complex to work with and are very expensive. The aim of this book is to present, in an easily referenced form for compound manufacturer, nutrition adviser and livestock producer alike, basic information about the different feeds they are likely to encounter in the mill or on the farm. My intention while writing was to categorise clearly the materials with which we work, so that the most appropriate selections can be made to meet the precise needs of the different nutritional situations with which we are faced.

I do not claim to have produced a definitive reference book, and no doubt there is information I have failed to identify and confidential, unpublished data to which I have no access. I have tried to draw together a brief description of many of the feeds potentially available in the UK, with the aim of providing a framework on which individuals can build their own information base to meet their own particular needs, and to which they can add from experience.

The text attempts to clarify the names of different feeds, particularly where confusion is known to occur, as with by-products from the distilling industry. I have also identified common features which characterise different groups of feed. The analytical data have been selected to describe each feed in a way that indicates the role to which it is best suited. It should allow the use of existing systems of feed evaluation and ration formulation, as well as some of those presently being developed which show potential for the future.

During the preparation of this book I have received numerous pieces of information and comments from many sources, and I am grateful to everyone who has helped me. I would, however, particularly like to thank Ian Givens and Jeannie Everington of the ADAS Feed Evaluation Unit for supplying information and discussing data, particularly regarding the carbohydrate fractions of feeds. I wish also to thank Dr Barbara Stark for her sterling efforts in keeping me writing, and for her constructive comments and editing of the script. The final responsibility for the information contained in this book, however, lies with me.

Chris Lonsdale
January 1989

STRAIGHTS

Raw Materials for Animal Feed Compounders and Farmers

by

Dr Chris Lonsdale

CHALCOMBE PUBLICATIONS

First published in Great Britain by
   Chalcombe Publications, 13 Highwoods Drive,
   Marlow Bottom, Marlow, Bucks SL7 3PU

February 1989

© C.R. Lonsdale 1989

ISBN 0 948617 15 2

Printed in Great Britain by Cambrian News Ltd, Aberystwyth

ABBREVIATIONS

BSE	Bovine Spongiform Encephalopathy
Ca	Calcium
CF	Crude fibre
cm	Centimetre
CP	Crude protein
DM	Dry matter
D value (DOMD)	Digestible organic matter in the dry matter
EE	Ether extract
EEC	European Economic Community
g	Gram
hl	Hectolitre
K	Potassium
kg	Kilogram
lb	Imperial pound
m^3	Cubic metre
ME	Metabolisable energy
Mg	Magnesium
mg	Milligram
μmol	Micromole
MJ	Megajoule
mm	Millimetre
N	Nitrogen
NA	Data not available
NaCl	Sodium chloride (salt)
NCD	Neutral detergent cellulase digestibility
NDF	Neutral detergent fibre
NFE	Nitrogen free extractive
NPN	Non-protein nitrogen
P	Phosphorus
RDP	Rumen degradable protein
Ssp	Subspecies
UDP	Ruminally undegradable dietary protein
VFA	Volatile fatty acids

Chapter 1

RAW MATERIALS FOR LIVESTOCK FEEDS

Many different raw materials have potential as feeds for livestock. In practice, two important questions must be asked before rations are formulated—which feed ingredients should be used and how much of each should be included? For effective use, the nutritive characteristics of the individual materials must be assessed, and then complementary combinations of the different straights selected to meet the dietary requirements of farm livestock by the most cost-effective means.

Rations for ruminant farm livestock are, in general, based on forages supplemented with other feeds to provide adequate levels of energy, protein, minerals and vitamins for the required type and level of production. The supplementary feeds most commonly offered are proprietary compounds, home mixes or straights, with root crops often making an important contribution to energy supply.

The many different potential feed materials available may be used as ingredients in proprietary compounds and/or directly on-farm. Feed ingredients include cereals and seeds which are grown specifically for the purpose, and a wide range of by-products from various processing industries. Within groups of ingredients such as cereal grains or oilseed meals, nutritional characteristics tend to be similar, but overall the raw materials available to feed to livestock cover a wide range of composition, nutritive value and nutritional characteristics.

A large number of very different livestock feeds arise during the processing and manufacture of human food and drink. For example, when seeds like soya bean or oilseed rape are crushed to expel their oil, the familiar, protein-rich soya bean and rapeseed meals are produced. In contrast, the residues of sugar extraction and refining, beet pulp and molasses respectively, are valuable energy sources—the former contains high levels of digestible fibre while the latter primarily comprises sugars, but neither contain significant amounts of protein. The cereal fractions remaining after the malting and mashing processes during brewing and distilling consist mainly of digestible fibre, but they also contain some protein.

To categorise and select different feeds requires the use of criteria which relate closely to the animal's nutrient requirements. The development of appropriate classification systems is of great importance to compounders and livestock producers alike, and their use is necessary for the cost-effective utilisation of feed resources, and therefore profitable animal production.

The high nutritive value of diets based on a variety of different feeds, each imparting its particular characteristics to the overall diet, was demonstrated by Bobby Boutflour and his colleagues in the 1940s. They offered dairy cows mixtures of cereals, cereal by-products and oilseed meals together with hay to support lactations approaching 9,000 litres. Since then, the average genetic potential of farm animals has increased and the choice of feeds available has broadened, but this situation is not always exploited to the full by the wise choice of dietary ingredients.

During the last decade the importance of selecting feeds for ruminants on the basis of specific nutritional features such as digestible fibre content, protein degradability and effect on appetite, as well as on their overall energy and protein content has been realised. The identification and selection of individual dietary ingredients which supply the right level and type of nutrients cost-effectively depend upon appropriate feed evaluation techniques and a sound knowledge of the principles of ruminant nutrition. Information on the composition and nutritive value of straights, together with *in vivo* data from feeding trials is needed so that animal performance can be predicted from laboratory assessments of individual samples.

In the UK, there is a legal requirement that certain information in the form of a statutory statement is given by any seller of animal feed to every buyer, but the information stipulated is not always particularly helpful in predicting the real nutritive worth of the material. In contrast, this book contains a range of information on the chemical composition and nutritional characteristics of many of the feed ingredients commonly available in the UK, to improve the effectiveness of selection of raw materials. The feeds are described both in terms of their overall nutrient content, and with reference to the type of energy yielding components and protein they supply. Information such as this is required to select the most appropriate combinations for different classes of livestock. A simplified index of the relative economic value of each straight feed is also given, to assist in assessing cost-effectiveness.

The detailed descriptions of the individual straights, given in Chapters 4 to 13, also cover their physical characteristics, as these may have important implications for the practicalities of their use. General information on the handling and storage of dry feeds, moist solids and liquids is provided in Chapter 3.

This book draws on many different sources of information as well as from the author's own experience, to give *typical* specifications for the broad range of feeds currently available in the U.K. It should, however, be noted that some data for the more recently available materials or for recently developed evaluation techniques are based on a very limited number of observations. In some instances specific data were not available to the author for individual raw materials, and this is denoted by "NA" in the descriptions of specific materials.

Raw materials vary according to their source and the exact processes to which they are subjected, therefore the values given in this book should be used only as a guide. Specific information about particular consignments should be sought from the supplier. When raw materials are known to be available in widely differing qualities some assurances about the specifications of the product being offered should be sought from the supplier before purchase.

CHAPTER 2

EVALUATION AND CLASSIFICATION OF FEED INGREDIENTS

Various systems of evaluating and classifying feeds have been used during the past 100 years, and continuing developments will bring further changes. The most commonly available information to describe feeds is based on their proximate analysis, that is crude protein (CP), ether extract (EE), crude fibre (CF) and ash contents, with differences between the sum of these and the total dry matter (DM) being termed the nitrogen free extractive (NFE). This relatively simple system of analysis, which was developed in Germany over 100 years ago, has in its day provided a useful description, but the fractions determined are rather general chemical groupings and are often not closely related to the nutritive value of feeds.

The most important nutritional features of most feeds are the amounts of usable energy and protein which they provide to various classes of livestock. Different raw materials supply these nutrients from different sources (substrates) and the levels and proportions of the various sources of energy and protein affect the way in which the feeds are digested, the products of digestion and therefore their overall nutritive value. The features which influence the way feeds are digested and their nutritive value to ruminants are described by Dr Bob Ørskov in *The Feeding of Ruminants**.

Dr Ørskov explains that in the large forestomach (the rumen) of ruminants there is a huge population of microorganisms that ferment feeds prior to digestion by the host animal. It has been understood for many years that fermentation produces organic acids (volatile fatty acids; VFA), which are absorbed from the rumen to be used as a source of energy by the host animal. The microorganisms themselves pass along the digestive tract to be digested by the host animal as a source of protein (microbial protein). We need to take account of the way in which feeds are digested (fermented) in the rumen and in the hind gut, and how this influences nutrient utilisation by the host animal.

Proximate analysis says little about the proportions of different carbohydrates or the type and quality of the protein present, and therefore little about the way a feed will be digested. It has long been recognised that crude fibre content is not an accurate predictor of the digestibility of a feed (i.e. the potentially useful portion). Digestibility can vary, for example with level of feeding, and the same digested nutrient is not necessarily used with equal efficiency by the animal for different purposes.

---

* Dr Bob Ørskov (1987) The Feeding of Ruminants. Chalcombe Publications, Marlow Bottom, Bucks.

During the late 1960s Van Soest, primarily with forages in mind, proposed a scheme of laboratory analysis to fractionate cell contents and cell wall constituents. This scheme, or modifications of it which use different types of detergent, is now widely used to give more meaningful characterisation of the carbohydrate fraction of feeds—that is the material contained within the crude fibre and nitrogen free extractive fractions of proximate analysis.

Possibly the most useful analytical parameter identified by Van Soest and his co-workers has been neutral detergent fibre (NDF), which appears to relate quite closely to the fibrous cell wall fraction of plant materials. This fraction is important because it contributes to dividing the carbohydrate content of plant material into rapidly and less rapidly digested portions which result in different mixtures of the end products of digestion. Sugars are digested most rapidly, then starch and most slowly, fibre.

Some of the measurements given in this book overlap with each other in the fractions of the feed which they identify, but broadly speaking the sum of sugar, starch, NDF, crude protein, oil and ash might be expected to account for most of the dry matter. For some feeds it does, but for others there is a significant shortfall. In most cases this difference can be explained by the presence of another category of carbohydrates, namely pectins, gums and mucilages. During chemical analysis these carbohydrates do not break down like sugars or starch and so they are not measured with them, but at the same time they are solubilised by neutral detergent solution and so are not measured as NDF. In the animal they are probably hydrolysed to yield mainly sugars, which are then digested as such.

Figure 2.1 illustrates the chemical composition of a varied selection of major feed types. This figure shows the extreme variation which exists and, importantly, how proportions of the different carbohydrate fractions vary as well as the contents of protein, oil and ash. Molasses, for example, contains predominantly sugar, whilst wheat comprises mainly starch, and unmolassed sugar beet pulp and brewers' grains have high contents of NDF (ie cell wall constituents).

Citrus and beet pulps contain substantial amounts of hitherto unclassified carbohydrates. The composition of brewers' grains demonstrates that moist feeds which contain potentially fermentable carbohydrates invariably have some of their energy-yielding dry matter in the form of volatile products of fermentation (volatile fatty acids or alcohols).

Whole soya beans demonstrate that oil content has a marked effect on energy value without substantially depressing protein content, whilst extracted rapeseed meal represents a typical oilseed meal. Fish meal is a widely accepted marine and animal protein standard, but the metabolisable energy content should be noted—protein has a higher energy value than carbohydrate.

5

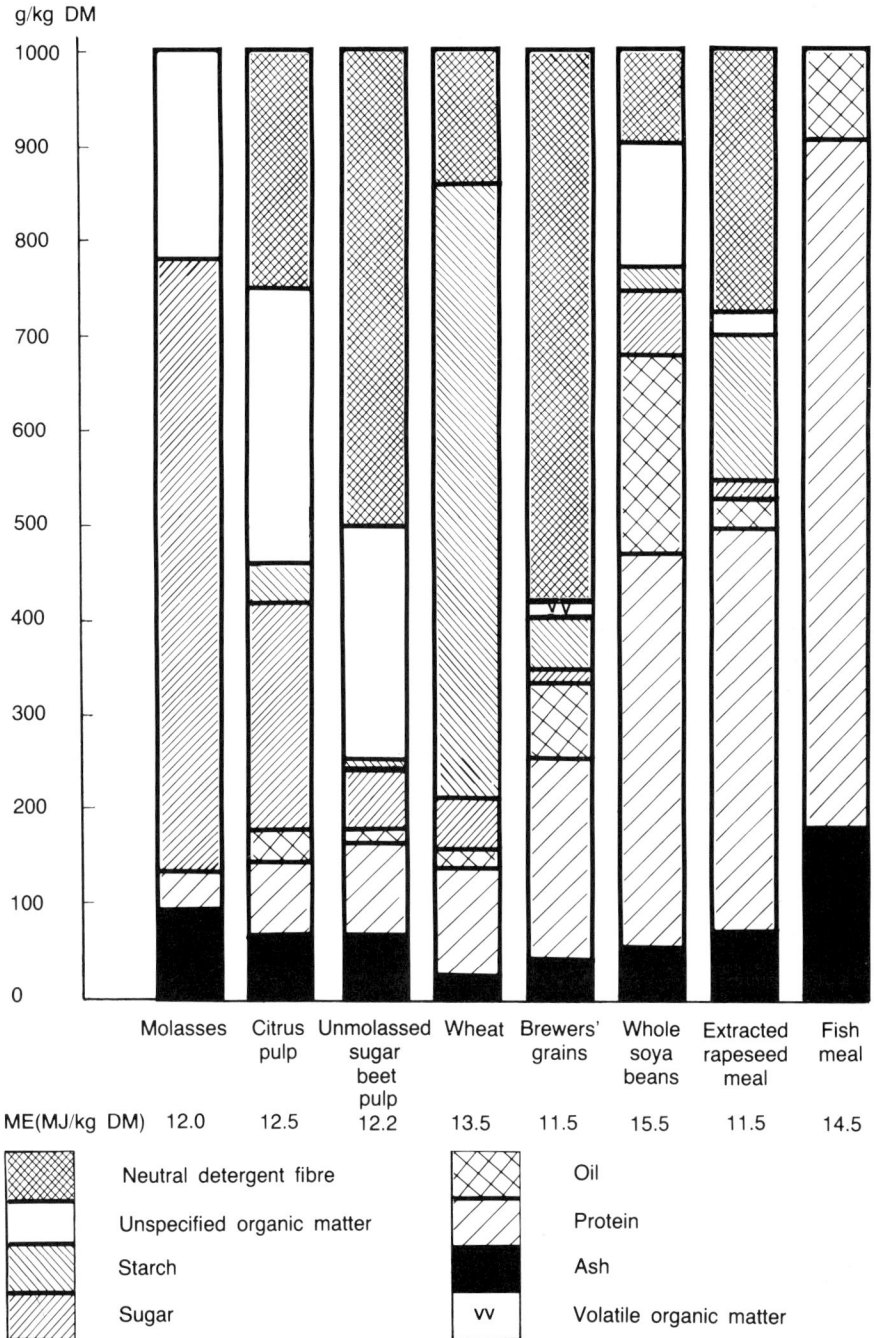

Figure 2.1 Composition of contrasting raw materials

g/kg DM

	Molasses	Citrus pulp	Unmolassed sugar beet pulp	Wheat	Brewers' grains	Whole soya beans	Extracted rapeseed meal	Fish meal
ME(MJ/kg DM)	12.0	12.5	12.2	13.5	11.5	15.5	11.5	14.5

Neutral detergent fibre

Unspecified organic matter

Starch

Sugar

Oil

Protein

Ash

vv Volatile organic matter

Energy

Metabolisable energy (ME) is used to describe the energy value of ruminant feeds in the UK. It is the total energy value of a feed minus that lost as indigestible feed residues (the faeces), as methane and as urine. For most practical purposes the metabolisable energy values of different feeds may be regarded as additive. The efficiency with which metabolisable energy is used is influenced by a number of animal and feed factors.

Metabolisable energy is most accurately determined by offering feeds to animals and measuring directly the different energy losses. The loss as methane is difficult to measure but for many feeds it is a relatively constant proportion of gross energy. In practice it is often calculated as *0.08 × gross energy.*

To determine metabolisable energy using *in vivo* feeding trials is time-consuming and expensive, consequently the assessment of metabolisable energy *in vivo* is only carried out on a limited number of samples, not on a routine basis. For many years there has been much interest in the development of simple, cheap and relatively rapid laboratory procedures for the routine determination of the metabolisable energy values of large numbers of samples.

Predictive equations based on proximate analysis necessitate generalised assumptions about the digestibility and energy yield of different fractions. They are not very accurate and demonstrate the inherent problems of trying to use results from simple chemical analyses to predict feeding value in a very complex digestive system. In the late 1950s/early 1960s an *in vitro* technique was developed at the then Grassland Research Institute (now the Institute for Grassland and Animal Production, Hurley) to simulate digestion in the ruminant. Material was incubated with a small quantity of rumen fluid, and then digested with acidified pepsin. Although developed initially to evaluate forages, this technique has a wider application.

The *in vitro* technique determines the content of digestible organic matter in the dry matter of a feed ("D" value or DOMD). From this metabolisable energy may be estimated. For example, MAFF (1984)* gives:

$$ME = 0.015 \times DOMD$$

where ME is expressed as MJ/kg DM, and DOMD as g/kg DM.

For greater accuracy the coefficient may be varied for different types of feed. *In vitro* determinations are easier and quicker than *in vivo* trials, but they still require specialised facilities and expertise, including the need to keep donor animals to provide rumen fluid. The "digestion" takes over 48 hours, thus several working days are required to assess and report on a sample.

---

*MAFF (1984) Energy Allowances and Feeding Systems for Ruminants. Reference Book 433. HMSO, London.

Typical D values are included in the present book as they are available for many raw materials, and their use is familiar to many nutritionists.

During the last decade a wide range of laboratory analyses have been examined for their ability to predict metabolisable energy content. In particular the Feed Evaluation Units of the Rowett Research Institute, Aberdeen, the Ministry of Agriculture, Fisheries and Food (MAFF) Agricultural Development and Advisory Service (ADAS), Drayton, and the Hannah Research Institute, Ayr, have studied relationships between laboratory measurements and metabolisable energy values determined directly.

Important factors influencing metabolisable energy content include the gross energy content, which is substantially influenced by the oil content and the type of carbohydrate present. Oil is important because its energy value is approximately twice that of carbohydrate or protein, and it is usually, but not invariably, well digested. In contrast, carbohydrates comprise a major part of many raw materials, and the digestibility of their more modest energy content is extremely variable. Of the three broad nutritional groups of carbohydrates the soluble fraction (sugars) is digested very rapidly, with fermentation being complete within an hour; the readily digested portion (primarily starch) is digested over a period of a few hours; and the structural or fibrous fraction (cell wall constituents) may only be partially digested after several days.

The data on individual feed ingredients contained in this book include starch and sugar contents, together with values for the contents of crude fibre and NDF. The crude fibre fraction of proximate analysis includes some but not all of the cellulose, hemicellulose and lignin present in feeds. Neutral detergent fibre determined by the method of Van Soest consists mainly of lignin, hemicellulose and cellulose. The oil content of feeds determined by proximate analysis is expressed as the quantity of material extractable in petroleum ether (now known as method A). Increasingly, acid hydrolysis is carried out before ether extraction (method B) to release certain constituents of the oil fraction, for example protected fats, which would otherwise remain undetected, but which may contribute substantially to the animal's energy supply.

In practice, the best estimates of metabolisable energy come from total gross energy content and digestibility of the dry matter. Neutral detergent cellulase digestibility (NCD) extends the determination of NDF by incubating the fibrous residues with the enzyme 'cellulase'. This recently developed technique is set to replace *in vitro* digestion as an evaluation and advisory tool. The NCD value is proving to be a useful guide to the energy content of different feeds for ruminants, although there are exceptions to its general application.

During the 1980s projects jointly funded by the UK Ministry of Agriculture, the National Farmers' Union (NFU) and the United Kingdom Agricultural Supply Trade Association (UKASTA) were conducted at the Rowett and Hannah Research Institutes to develop an equation to predict the metabolisable energy content of *compound* feeds. Results of studies using sheep and dairy cows were used to produce the following equation:

$$ME = 0.025 \text{ oil} + 0.014 \text{ NCD}$$

where ME is expressed as MJ/kg DM, oil content as g/kg DM and NCD as g/kg DM.

The composition of mixtures of feeds as found in compounds will be less extreme than the composition of the individual ingredients, and interactions between different feed characteristics in mixtures result in a generalised and possibly more predictable effect than that for individual ingredients. Equations developed for mixtures of feeds are not necessarily applicable to individual raw materials, nor to mixtures which contain a high proportion of one single ingredient. The metabolisable energy content of individual raw materials is still best estimated by *in vivo* trials or from relationships specifically developed for particular classes of ingredient.

Protein

Dietary proteins provide animals with amino acids with which to build their own proteins for lean meat, foetal tissues, milk or wool. Amino acids for ruminants are supplied either from microbial protein synthesis in the rumen, or from feed proteins which pass "undegraded" through the rumen to be digested and absorbed in the abomasum and small intestine. Protein which is neither attacked by rumen microorganisms nor digested by the animals' own enzymes (i.e. undegradable and indigestible) is of no nutritional value.

The microorganisms of the rumen degrade some dietary protein (rumen degradable protein; RDP) and use non-protein nitrogen (NPN) in the diet to synthesise their own tissue. Non-protein nitrogen may occur naturally as nitrates, amines and other other compounds in raw materials, or it may be added, for example as urea, by the feed producer. The crude protein content of a feed is, by definition, total nitrogen (N) content multiplied by 6.25 (based on an average of 16 percent nitrogen in protein). It includes non-protein nitrogen as well as the nitrogen in true protein. Ruminants utilise much of the non-protein nitrogen in the diet, but the balance between nitrogen available in the rumen and proteins or amino acids reaching the small intestine may be important.

A shortage of RDP may restrict rumen microbial activity and thus limit the supply of energy as well as protein to the animal. On the other hand, for ruminants of high productive potential, some high quality undegradable dietary protein (UDP) is necessary to supplement the microbial supply, which may be limiting in some way.

The proportion of a feed protein which is degraded in the rumen varies with the physical or chemical properties of the feed and with rumen conditions. The degradability of protein in a feed (i.e. the proportion of the protein which is broken down in the rumen) is not therefore an absolute value and may vary, usually within a limited range for any one raw material. An indication of degradability is useful to group proteins into broad categories to improve the effectiveness of ration formulation. In this guide, protein sources are assigned to one of four categories, with degradabilities covering the following ranges:

Category	Degradability
A	0.71 to 0.90
B	0.51 to 0.70
C	0.31 to 0.50
D	Less than 0.31

Degradability may be determined in several ways but it is often estimated from samples suspended in dacron bags in the rumen for measured periods of time. The values given are only a guide to the probable supply of UDP and RDP when a feed is given to a ruminant animal.

Classification of feeds based on energy and protein content

In practice, energy is usually the first limiting nutrient for farm animals and protein the second. Selection of feed ingredients will therefore be primarily on the basis of the energy and protein they provide, viewed in the context of how much they cost.

When formulating rations, situations often arise in which an ingredient is sought to raise the energy content when other constraints are met, or to raise the level or quality of the protein without reducing the overall energy content. To help in the initial selection of feeds to fulfill different roles, the raw materials described in this book have been classified as having high, medium and low levels of energy and high, medium or low protein contents.

Using this approach, a two-way table (Table 2.1) has been constructed as a guide to classifying different feeds. Within each of the nine categories, feeds have been listed in descending order of their typical protein content and the degradability category of that protein is indicated.

Minerals and vitamins

Dietary mineral and vitamin supply is best considered once the ration has been formulated to meet energy and protein requirements. As there are marked variations in the amounts of the major minerals provided by different raw materials, it is always worthwhile assessing the natural dietary supply in relation to animal requirements to select the most appropriate and cost-effective supplement. The provision of a mineral and vitamin supplement is not a major expense in relation to the other dietary ingredients, and there are considerable health and therefore economic benefits in avoiding mineral and vitamin deficiencies or imbalances.

Typical calcium (Ca), phosphorus (P), magnesium (Mg) and salt (NaCl) levels are given for each feed ingredient described in this book. Potassium (K) is rarely a limiting mineral, but typical potassium contents are given to help to avoid unduly high levels in

TABLE 2.1 Classification of raw materials according to their energy and protein
contents. The degradability of the protein is also indicated[1]

| Protein content (g/kg DM) | Metabolisable energy content (MJ/kg DM) | | |
	High >12.0	Medium 12.0 to 9.0	Low <9.0
High >200	Blood meal **D** Fishmeal **D** Maize gluten meal (prairie meal) **B** Poultry offal meal **B/C** Meat meal **C** Groundnut cake **A** Soya bean meal **B** Sesame meal **B** Soya beans (whole processed) **C** Condensed corn steep liquor Lupins (sweet) **B** Pot ale syrup **A** Linseed meal **B** Spent wash syrups **A** US corn distillers' dark grains **C** Beans (field) **C** Wheat distillers' dark grains **C** Malt distillers' dark grains **C** Peas **B** Delactosed whey syrup Copra expeller **B** Maize gluten feed **B**	Feather meal (hydrolysed) **D** Meat and bone meal **C** Rapeseed meal **B** Sunflower seed meal **B** Cottonseed cake **B** Safflower meal **A** Malt culms **B** Brussel sprout packhouse waste **A** Malt residual pellets **B** Brewers' grains **B** Palm kernel meal (extr.) **B**	Cotton cake (undec.) **B** Sunflower seed meal (undec.) **B** Safflower meal expeller **A**
Medium 200 to 120	Maize germ meal **B** Whey **A** Triticale **A** Wheat **A**	Wheat bran **B** Dried forages (grass, lucerne) **B** Wheatfeed **A**	Rice bran **C** Shea nut meal **D** Illipe meal **D**
Low <120	Barley **A** Oats **A** Sugar beet pulp (molassed, dried, pressed, ensiled) **B** Potatoes **A** Maize grain **B** Carrots **A** Citrus pulp **B** Molasses **A** Manioc **B**	Pectin extracted fruit **B** Apple pomace **B**	Oatfeed **C**

[1] Degradability: Category A = 0.71 to 0.90, B = 0.51 to 0.70, C = 0.31 to 0.50, D = less than 0.31

the diet. Molasses and blends of molasses and condensed molasses solubles are examples of feeds supplying high levels of potassium, which have been associated with scouring in ruminants.

Relative value index

As traders and buyers know all too well, the absolute and relative costs of different feeds are always changing and any economic value ascribed to a feed at a specific point in time is of limited use. In practice, values are often determined using linear programming and an assessment of the likely forward market movements. To compare the value of different raw materials within the context of this book, the slightly restrictive technique of evaluating each feed against two standards has been used.

The traditional standards of barley grain and soya bean meal have been used. Barley grain with a dry matter content of 860 g/kg, containing 12.9 MJ ME/kg DM and 117 g/kg DM crude protein, has been assigned a value of 100 units per tonne and soya bean meal (44/7), with a dry matter content of 890 g/kg, containing 13.3 MJ ME/kg DM and 480 g/kg DM crude protein, a value of 145 units per tonne.

Using the technique of solving simultaneous equations, partial values for a megajoule (MJ) of metabolisable energy and one gram of crude protein have been calculated and applied to the energy and crude protein contents given for each feed ingredient. The product of this calculation has been termed the relative value index, which in this guide is given on a fresh weight basis. The same exercise may be conducted using the actual cost of barley grain and soya bean meal at any point in time, to allow simple comparisons of the relative values of different feeds, to establish in broad terms whether they represent good value for money or not.

The following illustrates the calculation of the relative value index of a feed:

Barley grain at 100 units per tonne fresh weight
Adjusted for 860 g DM/kg ≡ 116.28 units per tonne DM.

Soya bean meal (SBM) at 145 units per tonne fresh weight
Adjusted for 890g DM/kg ≡ 162.92 units per tonne DM.

Expressed as mathematical equations:

$$\text{Barley} \quad 12.9\ ME + 117\ CP = 116.28 \quad (1)$$
$$\text{SBM} \quad 13.3\ ME + 480\ CP = 162.92 \quad (2)$$

Barley equation adjusted to have a common term with SBM (ie × 1.0310):

$$13.3\ ME + 120.63\ CP = 119.88$$

Solving equations (i.e. subtracting (3) from (2)):

$$359.37\ CP = 43.04$$

$$\text{Partial value per unit } CP = \frac{43.04}{359.37} = 0.1198$$

Substituting CP into equation (1) or (2) gives:

$$\text{Partial value per unit } ME = 7.9273$$

Relative value index

Manioc typically contains 12.8 MJ ME/kg DM and 30 g CP/kg DM, with a DM content of 800g/kg.

Relative value index on DM basis = 12.8 × 7.9273 + 30 × 0.1198 = 105.0634

Adjusted for material at 880 g DM/kg = 105.0634 × 0.880 = 92.4558

Relative value index for manioc (fresh weight basis) = 92.5

CHAPTER 3

HANDLING AND STORING RAW MATERIALS

Raw materials fall into three easily recognised categories according to their physical characteristics, namely liquids, moist solids and dry solids. The same general principles apply to the handling and storage of feeds within the same category. Dry solids in various forms are traditionally stored and handled both by the compounder and on the farm. Moist solids are really only suited to farm use while liquids, principally molasses but more recently fats, distillery syrups and milk processing by-products, are handled in bulk both in the compound mill and, if justified by the scale of use, on farm.

Liquids

Liquids available for feeding to livestock range from materials like fresh whey and skimmed milk, which have handling characteristics similar to those of water, to thick, viscous liquids such as cane molasses and distillery syrups. Liquids are available in bulk and are best handled as such for both physical and economic reasons.

Liquids are not the most convenient materials to handle in the feed mill and traditionally only molasses or blends of molasses and molasses condensed solubles have been used. Their handling characteristics are well investigated and understood, and manufacturers are wary of using other liquids which may exhibit different characteristics or be available in less consistent supplies. The relatively high nutritive values of some of the alternative materials now available suggest that their potential handling qualities should be examined, if not alone then perhaps in blends with molasses. In the case of oils, development of methods for liquid application in the mill has allowed greater use, for example by surface spraying. Molasses is traditionally used on the farm, and in addition some liquids which may not suit compound mills have been used directly by livestock producers. Delactosed whey syrup and pot ale syrup are examples.

Suitable tanks for liquids can be obtained relatively cheaply. Their size should be adequate to take 10 or 20 tonne deliveries. This means that, ideally, they should have a capacity of 12 or 23/24 tonnes so that a delivery can be made while the tank still holds several days' supply. This avoids last minute ordering and the risk of running out before the delivery is made. Large mills with a high throughput will use large tanks but smaller installations will generally be more suited to on-farm use.

Delivery tankers are usually fitted with a compressor or other pumping device so that elevated tanks can be erected from which distribution can then be by gravity. Obviously, if a pump is installed tanks may be sited at, or even below, ground level.

Wherever a tank is sited, it should be ventilated to avoid condensation forming on the inside of the roof of the tank and dripping onto the stored material. In addition to reducing the dry matter content by an unknown amount, when no preservative is present dilute materials are less stable than concentrated ones. The dilute surface layer which can be caused by condensation may be a starting point for fermentation or mould development.

When considering the specifications of a tank, note must be taken of the full range of liquids which might be stored in it, when calculating both a suitable volume and, where appropriate, the strength of supports. For example 23 tonnes of whey would require a capacity of about 23,000 litres (5,100 gallons) as its density is similar to that of water, about 1 kg per litre (10 lb per gallon). By contrast, the same tank filled with a delactosed whey syrup with a density 1.18 kg per litre (12 lb per gallon) would contain over 27 tonnes of material. Further, if the tank were filled with cane molasses with a density of 1.4 kg per litre (14 lb per gallon) the weight contained would be nearly 33 tonnes, which would require a load-bearing strength almost 50 percent greater than that needed for whey.

The range of liquids to be used as feeds also influences the specification of the plumbing to be installed. Pipes and valves little larger than those used for a domestic water supply are adequate for very fluid liquids, but viscous materials such as cane molasses require pipes and valves with internal diameters of 10 cm to 15 cm (4 inches to 6 inches).

On farm, liquids can be dispensed to animals in a variety of ways, and again their viscosity may influence the choice. One approach is to offer liquids alone in open troughs, by ball and wheel feeders or from dribble bars. A second approach is to provide the liquid with another feed. A small tractor-mounted tank can be filled from the main storage tank and material can be dispersed along a feed fence by means of a side-mounted delivery tube, the flow of liquid being controlled from the cab. The liquid may be dispersed on top of other feeds such as silage, brewers' grains or straw. Neat, convenient tanks are available for this purpose, designed for use with a quick action, rear tractor mounting. Alternatively, small distribution tanks have been successfully installed on forage boxes to discharge their contents into a feeding trough at the same time as solid feed is delivered from the main body of the box. Liquids have also been run onto the top of the contents of a forage box to form a layer just before delivery into the feeding trough, and they may also be easily added to complete diet feeders during the preparation of the feed.

The number of liquid feeds available is increasing, and at any one time some usually offer very good value for money. The existence on-farm of a facility to handle, store, and feed liquids is a valuable asset and is likely to remain so.

Moist solids

Moist feeds are essentially products to be handled, stored and used on-farm. In addition to the familiar brewers' grains and pressed beet pulp, this group contains more recently available forms of moist feeds from distilling or the wet milling of maize, and more locally available materials such as by-products from potato processing, and apple pomace. The dry matter of materials ranges from about 10 percent for late/early season apple pomace to over 40 percent for some of the newer distillery products. All are delivered in bulk, that is in 10 to 20 tonne loads which are tipped into suitable locations on the farm.

Moist solids can be subdivided into two broad types according to their storage and handling characteristics: those with sufficient residual, fermentable carbohydrate to ensile in a conventional manner and those which require a preservative to give them reasonable stability on-farm. Whichever type of material is stored, the most important single factor is to exclude air. The development of stable, acidic conditions preserves material in a purpose-built silo, ensiled alone or under forage, and correctly sealed with a polythene sheet. When the silo is opened, little deterioration should occur providing disturbance to the open face is minimised and exposed material is fed within a couple of days.

Even when loads are not conventionally ensiled as they are intended for immediate use, it is still well worth consolidating the surface layer to exclude air and to retard its rate of penetration into the mass. If a sheet is put over the stored material it should be in contact with the entire surface and weighted evenly over the whole area. Throwing sheets loosely over moist solids often results in condensation forming on the under-sides of the sheets, and dripping onto the material, thus encouraging rapid deterioration due to moulding.

In some cases the shelf life of moist products has been prolonged by the surface application of an acid silage additive. Enzyme-based silage additives may also protect the surface of some moist solids.

Mould spores are always present in a farm situation and practices which reduce the risk of them invading and thriving in moist feeds are worth employing. Mouldy feeds should be handled as little as possible and not offered to animals. While some moulds are relatively harmless, other species can cause considerable problems, such as farmers lung in humans or mycotic abortion in animals. In addition to risks to health, moulding wastes feed.

Dry solids

Traditionally, many raw materials and by-products have been made available in a dried form, either achieved naturally or as a result of further processing. Drying, or more importantly removing moisture, imparts a high degree of stability to raw materials. Most microorganisms, whether moulds, bacteria or yeasts, cannot grow without a minimum level of available moisture. Thus, it is most important that dried materials are kept dry if they are to remain wholesome; that means sound floors to prevent moisture rising from the ground, and sound roofs to prevent rain getting in. This requirement is the same whether the product is bagged or in bulk. Dampness will not only introduce risks of the development of harmful organisms and a reduction in feeding value, but will also result in material which is difficult to handle and could bridge in situations where that is a potential problem.

Dry products may be delivered in a variety of forms from those which have a significant content of difficult, fine, dusty material, for example some tapioca or imported dried lucerne products, through a range of meals and pelleted materials to well-formed pellets and nuts, such as those of dried molassed sugar beet pulp or some supplies of malt residual pellets.

It is, of course, important not only to establish the nutritive characteristics of an unfamiliar product but also in what form it will be delivered. Whether a product can be blown, whether it is likely to bridge in hoppers, whether its angle of repose is accommodated by the angles in the storage bins or whether it is likely to cause dust problems are important facts for both compounders and farmers.

CHAPTER 4

CEREALS

The use of by-products and cheaper alternatives to cereals in livestock feeds has increased during the last few years, but cereal grains are still important raw materials. On occasions the European Economic Community (EEC) Commission debates the possibility of subsidising an increased use of cereals in animal feeds, but it seems virtually impossible to propose a viable non-discriminating scheme.

As with other potential ingredients, the level at which cereals are included in animal feeds is determined to a large extent by the cost, relative to alternative materials, of the energy and protein which they supply. Relative cost influences both the quantity of cereal used in the feed mill or on-farm, and also the ratios in which different cereal grains are used. For example, when the cost of a tonne of wheat is similar to that of barley, wheat offers better value for money because of its higher energy and protein contents. Maize, despite having the highest energy value of all cereal grains, is sparingly used in Europe because of its high price.

Maize, wheat, triticale and a few recently bred varieties of oats have 'naked' grains; this means that they separate from their fibrous coats during threshing and the outer layer of the resulting grain is a thin skin of fused testa and pericarp. The overall fibre content of these grains is very low. Most varieties of barley and oats have 'clothed' grains, which means that after threshing they are still enclosed by two fibrous layers—the palea and lemma. Consequently, oats in particular, but also barley contain more fibre and less starch than the other three cereal grains described. Overall, fibrousness increases in the following order: maize, wheat, triticale, naked oats, barley and oats. Starch contents and metabolisable energy values for ruminants decrease in the same order. Protein content tends to be highest for triticale, decreasing progressively for wheat, barley, naked oats, oats and maize.

Cereals are included in rations primarily as a source of energy, which is present mainly as starch. The starch grains of different cereals vary slightly in size and chemical structure so that their patterns of digestion differ to some extent. Sheep can utilize whole cereals well, but the grains should be cracked or rolled when fed to cattle. Overprocessing should be avoided as grinding, for example, can reduce digestibility. For ruminants heat treatments such as steaming and micronisation are of limited value because the marginal improvement in nutritive value does not always cover the cost of processing.

A high proportion of the dry matter of all cereals is rapidly fermented in the rumen, thus cereals should be introduced gradually to the diet and eventually fed either in limited quantities during discrete feeds, or made available on a continuous 24-hour basis to avoid excessive intakes at any one time. As oats have a higher fibre content that the other cereals, they are fermented in the rumen at a slower rate and thus tend to be regarded as a "safer" feed. Triticale is not yet commonly available but, due to its higher protein content combined with a high metabolisable energy value, it may be a useful feed ingredient in the future.

The following tables give typical data for five cereals—barley, maize, oats, triticale and wheat. This information may be used both to assess the cereals as livestock feeds and as a reference against which other raw materials may be considered.

Feed	**BARLEY**	*High energy : low protein*

Description

Barley (*Hordeum sativum* Pers.) is a cereal grown predominantly in temperate regions. Its height is 40 to 120 cm depending on variety and growing conditions. The flowers and grain are borne in a dense spike. The grain is used mainly in the brewing and distilling industries, in addition to being an animal feed.

Physical form

The elongated grain is usually slightly angular, with an awn. After threshing the clothed grain remains sheathed in two fibrous layers -the lemma (outer) and palea (inner). Both ends of the grain are truncated—where it was originally attached to the rachis (central stalk) and where the awn was attached before threshing. Its colour ranges from straw-like to pale yellow. 1000 grain weight averages about 42 gram with a typical range of 35 to 45 gram.

Bulk density

630 to 670 kg/m^3 (mean value 650 kg/m^3 or 65 kg/hl). Bushel weight 50 to 58 lb (mean 54 lb).

DM content

860 g/kg

Typical nutritional specification (gram per kg DM except for energy)

ME (MJ/kg DM)	12.9	Crude protein	117
D value	820	Oil (method A)	13
NCD	NA	Oil (method B)	NA
NDF	230	Calcium	1.1
Crude fibre	50	Phosphorus	3.9
Starch	530	Magnesium	1.2
Sugar	35	Salt	1.0
Ash	31	Potassium	5.0

Nutritional comments

Barley is perhaps the cereal most widely used in ruminant feeds in the UK and the intensive cereal beef system developed in the early 1960s was based on it. Despite being a clothed grain, the fibre content of barley is not particularly high and the grain is rapidly fermented in the rumen. Ingestion of large amounts in one feed or too rapid introduction into the ration may lead to bloat and/or acidosis, which in some cases may be fatal.

Availability

Barley is usually available throughout the year but, if the market is particularly weak, growers or merchants may be reluctant to sell.

Relative value index

Barley has been assigned a value of 100 which, together with the value of 145 assigned to soya bean meal, has been used to calculate the 'relative value index' for the other feeds described.

| Feed | **MAIZE** | | *High energy : low protein* |

Description

Maize (*Zea mays* L.), also known as "Indian corn" or "corn" is a large, coarse cereal grown in most countries where the summers are long and warm. Its height can exceed 2 metres. Several spikes, taking the form of 'Corn on the cob', are borne in the leaf axils of each plant. Where summers are inadequate to ripen the grain, as in much of the UK, the whole plant may be harvested as a forage feed. The grain is processed extensively for its starch content and it is used for distilling as well as for animal feeds. Recently its relatively high price in the UK has severely reduced its use in distilling and as a feed ingredient. Whole maize grains are now rarely used in ruminant diets, except in the flaked form in some coarse rations for young calves.

Physical form

Maize grains are large, bold, hard, flinty and about the size of a garden pea. They range in colour from deep golden yellow to almost white.

Bulk density

DM content

870 g/kg (range 865 to 885 g/kg)

Typical nutritional specification (gram per kg DM except for energy)

ME (MJ/kg DM)	13.8	Crude protein	100
D value	880	Oil (method A)	40
NCD	NA	Oil (method B)	NA
NDF	109	Calcium	0.2
Crude fibre	20	Phosphorus	3.0
Starch	700	Magnesium	1.2
Sugar	11	Salt	0.2
Ash	20	Potassium	3.2

Nutritional comments

Maize has the highest ME content of the cereals reviewed here, and the starch it contains is digested slightly more slowly in the rumen than that of wheat or barley. At high levels of feeding the starch can pass undigested from the rumen into the small intestine. Maize is therefore slightly more suited than wheat or barley as a feed for ruminants, but its advantage is rarely sufficient to justify its higher cost. Like other cereal grains, excess energy is provided in relation to protein and a supplementary source of protein is necessary to exploit the full nutritive value of maize.

Availability

Generally available throughout the year, but trade is affected by relative cost.

Relative value index

105.6

Feed	**OATS**		*High energy : low protein*	

Description Oats (*Avena sativa* L.) are stout plants which grow up to 1 metre high. The whole oat plant may be harvested during the leafy growth stage to use as a forage. Alternatively the grain, which is carried in loose, open panicles, may be harvested when mature and ripe. In practice, oats tend to be grown either under contract for the manufacture of human food products or for direct use on the farm. They are not a widely grown cereal in the UK, and their use in compound feeds is limited, although because of their fibrous nature they are the most suitable cereal for horse feeds. At the right price and, if available, they could be useful to produce higher fibre diets for ruminants.

Physical form The grain is a clothed seed, with 1000 grains typically weighing 35 to 40 gram. The usual colour lies between very pale cream and straw. The grains are elongated and about 12 mm long, with the end which was attached to the stalk slightly truncated.

Bulk density 500 to 560 kg/m^3. Bushel weight 40 to 45 lb.

DM content 850 g/kg

Typical nutritional specification (gram per kg DM except for energy)

ME (MJ/kg DM)	12.0	Crude protein	110
D value	665	Oil (method A)	40
NCD	NA	Oil (method B)	NA
NDF	320	Calcium	0.8
Crude fibre	100	Phosphorus	3.5
Starch	470	Magnesium	1.0
Sugar	15	Salt	0.5
Ash	20	Potassium	6.0

Nutritional comments Oat grains are only just classified as a 'high energy' feed as they are much more fibrous than other cereals grown in the UK. Oats are traditionally used for horses because of their high fibre content, but at the right price they are a potential ingredient in higher fibre diets for dairy cows.

Availability Oats are not often traded as most are either grown under contract or for use by the grower for his own animals.

Relative value index 92.1

Feed	**TRITICALE**	*High energy : medium protein*

Description Triticale (*Triticum* × *Secale*) was bred in an attempt to combine the characteristics of its parents—wheat and rye. The cereal has been developed commercially since the mid-1960s, when it appeared that it was possible to breed strains which exhibited the yield potential of wheat together with some of the hardiness and tolerance of rye. It has been shown that, in Europe, triticale can outyield most cereals, particularly on light soils.

Physical form Triticale has a naked grain, resembling wheat.

Bulk density 720 kg/m^3

DM content 860 g/kg

Typical nutritional specification (gram per kg DM except for energy)

ME (MJ/kg DM)	13.8	Crude protein	135
D value	875	Oil (method A)	18
NCD	NA	Oil (method B)	NA
NDF	NA	Calcium	1
Crude fibre	25	Phosphorus	4.5
Starch	540	Magnesium	1.2
Sugar	30	Salt	0.9
Ash	20	Potassium	5

Nutritional comments Triticale is a naked grain with a high energy value and moderate protein content which combines the characteristics of wheat and rye. Nutritionally it is an attractive feed and has given good results in a limited number of feeding trials. It is similar to wheat but its quality can be more variable, particularly its protein content (110 to 160 g/kg DM). Some tests have suggested that the grain may contain slightly greater contents of trypsin inhibitor and alkyl resorcinols than other cereals, but this should not be a problem for ruminants. Unfortunately it has inherited a susceptability to ergot from rye, and consignments must be cleared free from ergot before they are used. Levels up to 25 or 30% in compound feeds for cattle and in other concentrate mixes appear to be acceptable.

Availability Small amounts are grown in the UK and it is not commonly available. The amount grown in Europe is slowly increasing and livestock producers may consider growing it for their own use.

Relative value index 108.0

Feed	**WHEAT**	*High energy : medium protein*

Description

Wheat (*Triticum aestivum* L. *T. vulgare* Vill) is grown extensively in temperate and cooler tropical countries. Modern varieties vary considerably in height. Some have been bred for short straw length, being less than 30 cm, whilst other varieties may reach over 1 metre in height. Wheat has been grown in Britain for over 4000 years, primarily for milling to produce flour for baking. Recently, wheat has been used by the starch processing industry and in distilling. When the price is favourable, wheat can be used extensively as a feed ingredient, particularly for pigs and poultry, but also in significant amounts for ruminants.

Physical form

The naked grain is bold and basically oval, with a truncated end edged by a brush line and a very prominent crease running its full length. The grain ranges from reddish to almost white in colour. Typically 1000 grain weight varies from 40 to 55 gram.

Bulk density

700 to 770 kg/m^3 (mean 735 kg/m^3 or 73.5 kg/hl). Minimum standard for intervention and many trade contracts is 68 kg/hl. Bushel weight 56 to 62 lb.

DM content

855 g/kg (range 840 to 890 g/kg)

Typical nutritional specification (gram per kg DM except for energy)

ME (MJ/kg DM)	13.5	Crude protein	120
D value	880	Oil (method A)	18
NCD	930	Oil (method B)	NA
NDF	130	Calcium	0.5
Crude fibre	25	Phosphorus	3.5
Starch	660	Magnesium	1.1
Sugar	55	Salt	0.5
Ash	24	Potassium	4.7

Nutritional comments

As a naked grain, wheat is characteristically high in starch and low in fibre , which needs to be taken into account when choosing the level of inclusion and complementary ration ingredients. Wheat contains high levels of gluten and excessive amounts, particularly if the grains are finely ground, can result in a sticky, doughy mass in the rumen, discomfort to the animal and digestive disturbances. An upper limit for use is usually considered to be 25% of the concentrate, but higher levels have been successfully fed. The ME and CP contents may vary from 11.5 to 14.5 MJ/kg DM, and from 100 to 155 g/kg DM, but typical values are between 13 and 14, and 115 and 125 respectively. Protein content in particular is influenced by the growing season.

Availability

With production tending to be greater than demand, some stored wheat is generally carried over from one year to the next, so this cereal is usually available all year.

Relative value index

103.8

CHAPTER 5

BY-PRODUCTS FROM CEREAL PROCESSING

Cereals provide the staple diet for many of the world's people, as well as being an important livestock feed in some areas. Cereals are consumed as a human food in many forms, ranging from the whole grain after separation from the rest of the plant, and grain processed simply such as by grinding or cooking, to individual fractions of the grain such as bran or cornflour, and products such as the iso-glucoses used in some soft drinks, which are produced by refining and subsequently converting maize starch. Most processing results in the production of by-products or residues which may be very useful as animal feeds.

Many of the cereal by-products and processing residues are broadly similar in nature, in that they contain the fibrous and/or protein portions of the original grain. All cereal by-products, like whole cereal grains, have a low calcium level relative to the phosphorus content.

Traditional dry milling, usually of wheat, produces flour, which consists principally of starch and is used mainly for baking. The variety of residues produced at different stages of the milling process are fibrous and contain relatively high levels of protein. Historically the residues have been known by different names, often varying with area or even from mill to mill. Similar fractions from different mills, for example, may have been known by different names. In recent years, however, it has become the practice to combine the various residues and to trade them as bran, fine wheatfeed or coarse wheatfeed. In fact the situation now is usually further reduced to considering only bran and straight run wheatfeed.

Modern roller mills are supplied with well-cleaned and conditioned wheat, blended to give the type of finished flour required. The different pairs of rollers (breaks) are designed progressively to break down the grain and allow different fractions to be separated. The process is extended by scalpers which separate the aleurone and endosperm from the bran, and flour bolters that separate fine fibre from flour. The total amount of residue produced approaches 30 percent of the original grain weight. Today, *bran* is rarely available as a feed for ruminants because it is used extensively to supply fibre in human food, with any surplus being used in rations for horses. *Wheatfeed*, which varies according to the nature of the original grist, and the amount (extraction rate) and the type of flour produced, is widely available for inclusion in animal feeds.

Oats are also milled during their preparation as a human food. The fibrous by-products are usually collected and distributed as *oatfeed*. In hot, wet parts of the world, particularly the Far East, rice is the staple cereal and it is processed to remove the fibrous outer layers of the grain. *Rice bran* is widely traded throughout the world as a low quality animal feed.

The other widely milled cereal of significance to the UK feed industry is maize. Milling is usually by a wet technique. Cracked, screened maize grain is first soaked (steeped) in a dilute solution of sulphur dioxide, then passed through a series of rollers, grinders and centrifuges which separate out the fibre, maize germ, gluten and starch fractions.

Corn steep liquor, from soaking the grain, is usually concentrated to about 50 percent dry matter by evaporation, to produce *condensed corn steep liquor (CCSL)* which may be used as a growth substrate in the pharmaceutical industry or as an animal feed, or it may be recombined with other by-products in the manufacture of maize gluten feed. Maize germs are either extracted or expelled to release their oil, and the residue (germcake) may be handled separately or, again, blended into maize gluten feed. Most of the gluten is processed separately to form a protein meal which is rich in natural yellow pigments—xanthophylls. This product is particularly useful in diets for laying hens.

The starch may be ground into cornflour or subjected to further processing in a glucose refinery.

Normal practice in the UK has been to dry the by-products of the wet milling of maize, to produce *maize germ meal, maize gluten meal* and *maize gluten feed.* Until recently, moist products became available to feed to animals only when the drying plant failed but, as in the distilling industry, the possibility of regular supplies of moist material has been examined. A moist product similar in dry matter composition to maize gluten feed has been available in parts of Holland for a year or two and now similar material is available in the UK.

It is important to distinguish between maize gluten, the high protein component of maize grain, and maize gluten feed, which is a more fibrous blend of several by-products. The term maize gluten is often used loosely for either.

The main by-products from processing maize, wheat, oats and rice are detailed, in alphabetical order, in the following pages.

Feed	**CONDENSED CORN STEEP LIQUOR**

High energy : high protein

Description
Steep liquor from the initial process in the wet milling of maize, which contains soluble constituents from the grain, is condensed by evaporation. The product, condensed corn steep liquor (CCSL), is palatable but tastes salty.

Physical form
This yellow/amber, viscous liquid tends to gel if allowed to stand and cool. Its pH is usually about 4.0.

Bulk density
1200 g/kg

DM content
500 g/kg

Typical nutritional specification (gram per kg DM except for energy)

ME (MJ/kg DM)	13.0	Crude protein	400
D value	720	Oil (method A)	10
NCD	NA	Oil (method B)	20
NDF	NA	Calcium	1
Crude fibre	—	Phosphorus	25
Starch	20	Magnesium	10
Sugar	170	Salt	10
Ash	180	Potassium	45

Nutritional comments
This by-product could usefully contribute protein to liquid feed preparations and to moist blends of maize by-products. Its level of use must be restricted because its potassium content is relatively high; large quantities of CCSL may severely affect the water balance of pigs and cause scouring in ruminants.

Availability
Currently CCSL is only available occasionally, but this could change if methods of handling moist maize by-products alter.

Relative value index
75.5

Feed	**MAIZE GERM MEAL**	*High energy : medium protein*

Description During the wet milling of maize, after the initial grinding the germs are removed whole. They are then dried and the oil is expelled or extracted, leaving either 'high' or 'low' oil maize germ meal which may be traded as a single commodity or blended with other by-products in maize gluten feed.

Physical form Maize germ meal is a pale yellow, slightly oily meal.

Bulk density

DM content 900 g/kg

Typical nutritional specification (gram per kg DM except for energy)

	High oil	Low oil		High oil	Low oil
ME (MJ/kg DM)	14.5	13.0	Crude protein	150	250
D value	800	770	Oil (method A)	120	40
NCD	NA	NA	Oil (method B)	NA	NA
NDF	NA	NA	Calcium	1	2
Crude fibre	80	110	Phosphorus	4	6
Starch	200	200	Magnesium	1	1
Sugar	8	10	Salt	1	1
Ash	30	35	Potassium	2	3

Nutritional comments Maize germ meal is a useful feed for all classes of livestock, particularly when high levels of energy are required. Meals with a high oil content, if used in large quantities, may result in soft fat in animals reared for meat. As with all maize products, the protein is of limited nutritive value in respect of its amino acid content. Up to 2 kg of maize germ meal per day for large beef animals or dairy cows is an acceptable level of inclusion in the diet. The precise level of use will be influenced by the other feeds, particularly of maize origin, which are included in the diet.

Availability Supplies are usually available throughout the year.

Relative value index High oil: 119.6; Low oil: 119.7

| Feed | **MAIZE GLUTEN FEED** | *High energy : high protein* |

Description

Maize gluten feed (MGF) is a mixture of corn steep liquor, maize fibre and maize germ meal arising from the wet milling of maize to extract its starch. Large amounts are imported from the USA but supplies are also available from processing plants in the UK which use imported maize.

Physical form

This feed is usually available as a pale straw to mid- brown dried product (meal or pellets), but it is occasionally available moist from UK processors. Imported material is usually mealy, as the pellets break down during handling and shipment. The modest oil content and inclusion of steep liquor reduces dustiness.

Bulk density

600 kg/m^3, varying with physical form.

DM content

880 to 900 g/kg

Typical nutritional specification (gram per kg DM except for energy)

ME (MJ/kg DM)	13.0	Crude protein	200
D value	770	Oil (method A)	30
NCD	NA	Oil (method B)	NA
NDF	390	Calcium	1
Crude fibre	80	Phosphorus	8
Starch	150	Magnesium	5
Sugar	15	Salt	5
Ash	50	Potassium	8

Nutritional comments

Like all cereal by-products, MGF is a milled product, thus the fibre content does not have the same effect in the rumen as does long fibre in forage. On average MGF is classified as high protein but some samples contain less than 200 g/kg protein. Heat treatment during production renders the protein, which does not have a very useful amino acid composition, relatively undegradable (category B). The overall digestibility of the protein is usually above 0.8 unless excessive heat damage during drying, indicated by a very dark brown colour, has occurred. Levels of MGF up to 4 kg daily for dairy cows are quite acceptable. Much higher levels have been successfully used, but there is a risk of an unbalanced diet and of reducing milk fat production and/or favouring weight gain rather than milk production. If used above 30% in rations for beef, cream or yellow fat may result.

Availability

Maize gluten feed is available all year but most is sold during the winter months. Large amounts from the USA keep the price competitive.

Relative value index

113.0

Feed	**MAIZE GLUTEN MEAL**	*High energy : high protein*

Description

After the fibrous outer layer and germ from the maize grain has been removed during wet milling, the residue is ground and the slurry centrifuged to separate the gluten from the starch. The gluten is usually dried to produce a product which is only moderately palatable if fed alone. One source of maize gluten meal is known as prairie meal.

Physical form

The granular meal is a bright golden yellow colour.

Bulk density

550 g/kg

DM content

890 g/kg

Typical nutritional specification (gram per kg DM except for energy)

ME (MJ/kg DM)	16.0	Crude protein	670
D value	920	Oil (method A)	25
NCD	980	Oil (method B)	NA
NDF	25	Calcium	0.5
Crude fibre	12	Phosphorus	4.5
Starch	155	Magnesium	0.5
Sugar	—	Salt	0.6
Ash	30	Potassium	1.0

Nutritional comments

As with maize grain, excessive use of maize gluten meal may lead to soft and creamy carcase fat. The xanthophyll content (150 to 300 mg/kg) which gives the characteristic coloration is very useful in the diets of laying hens to deepen the yolk colour, but may adversely affect carcase fat colour. Although high in protein, the amino acid composition is not particularly good and the degradability category is only B. Diets containing a significant quantity of maize protein may need supplementary lysine and tryptophan, particularly with highly productive livestock. These particular characteristics of maize gluten meal mean that it is rarely considered for ruminant diets.

Availability

Limited quantities are available throughout the year. Maize gluten meal is in demand for use in poultry diets, and does not usually represent good value for money in ruminant rations.

Relative value index

184.3

Feed	**OATFEED**	*Low energy : low protein*

Description

Oatfeed consists of a mixture of the by-products arising during the milling of oats to produce oatmeal for human consumption. Its characteristics vary according to the actual amounts of screenings, husk and mealy/floury material included. Overall, oatfeed is of low nutritive value but to prevent it containing excessive amounts of very low quality husk, the feeding stuffs legislation defines an overall maximum crude fibre content of 270 g/kg (300 g/kg DM) for oatfeed. Oat husk (hulls) alone contain about 350 g/kg DM crude fibre.

Physical form

Oatfeed is a finely ground, fibrous meal.

Bulk density

DM content

900 g/kg

Typical nutritional specification (gram per kg DM except for energy)

ME (MJ/kg DM)	6.0	Crude protein	35
D value	40	Oil (method A)	15
NCD	NA	Oil (method B)	NA
NDF	NA	Calcium	2
Crude fibre	300	Phosphorus	2
Starch	40	Magnesium	1
Sugar	10	Salt	1
Ash	40	Potassium	8

Nutritional comments

Oatfeed is a fibrous product of low nutritive value, suited only to ruminant diets. It should be used sparingly in rations for highly productive animals so that the overall energy value of the diet is not too low. Adding fibre to ruminant diets in a finely milled form like oatfeed will not have the same effect as fibre consumed as forage which has not been finely processed. The protein in oatfeed is classed as C degradability, but the overall digestibility is so low that the product has virtually no useful protein value. The apparent digestibility of the protein is usually listed as zero.

Availability

A little oatfeed is available throughout the year, but most material is traded through well-established routes.

Relative value index

46.6

| Feed | RICE BRAN (EXTRACTED) | *Low energy : medium protein* |

Description

The threshed grain of rice (*Oryza sativa* L.) is enclosed in a siliceous and fibrous outer husk and a layer of bran (glume). The first stage of processing rice is to remove the hull to reveal brown rice. The first stage of milling is the removal of the bran using rapidly revolving abrasive cones; this may be continued to remove the aleurone layer and germ, producing pearl or polished rice. The bran contains 140 to 180 g/kg oil which, if not extracted, will go rancid, thus extracted rice bran is the product most usually traded in Europe. A crude fibre content above 200 g/kg DM would suggest that husk had been added to the bran.

Physical form

Rice bran is a light brown to silver coloured fibrous meal.

Bulk density

DM content

880 g/kg

Typical nutritional specification (gram per kg DM except for energy)

ME (MJ/kg DM)	7.0	Crude protein	160
D value	460	Oil (method A)	10
NCD	NA	Oil (method B)	NA
NDF	360	Calcium	2
Crude fibre	175	Phosphorus	14
Starch	310	Magnesium	7
Sugar	10	Salt	2
Ash	160	Potassium	9

Nutritional comments

Straight rice bran is a useful ingredient in ruminant feeds, provided that it is not included at too high a level so that the ME content of the mix is too low. If the fibre and ash levels are much greater than those given above, adulteration with rice hulls should be suspected and an even lower nutritive value expected, particularly in respect of energy levels. Blends of rice hulls and bran are much inferior to bran itself and should be refered to as *rice mill feeds*. Unextracted rice bran, with its full complement of oil, has a higher energy value than extracted bran but high levels of use could lead to soft fat and there would be a risk of rancidity from lipolytic enzyme activity. Rancid bran is not readily consumed, and its use could result in normal levels of dietary vitamin E being insufficient.

Availability

Rice bran is traded throughout the year.

Relative value index

65.7

| **Feed** | **WHEAT BRAN** | *Medium energy : medium protein* |

Description

When milling wheat the effect of the initial shearing rollers (first break) is broadly to separate the outer fibrous layers from the rest of the grain and the germ. Bran consists predominantly of the husk (pericarp and testa, or coarse bran) and the thin papery layer from around the starch (aleurone, or fine bran). Very little starch (endosperm) is found in bran.

Physical form

Wheat bran is a fibrous, flaky product.

Bulk density

DM content   880 g/kg

Typical nutritional specification (gram per kg DM except for energy)

ME (MJ/kg DM)	10.6	Crude protein	175
D value	600	Oil (method A)	42
NCD	NA	Oil (method B)	NA
NDF	500	Calcium	1
Crude fibre	120	Phosphorus	12
Starch	180	Magnesium	6
Sugar	40	Salt	1
Ash	70	Potassium	5

Nutritional comments

Wheat bran is a low density, flaky ingredient which has traditionally been used to lighten meals and make them more 'open'. When available, it is an excellent ingredient in coarse mixes for young growing ruminants. It is palatable and has a characteristic wheaty smell. The protein is relatively digestible (coefficient about 0.75) and categorised as B degradability. Fibre and ME contents vary slightly depending on the specification of the wheat being milled and the exact processes used in the mill, as these factors affect the overall blend of bran components. Crude fibre content may vary from 100 to 130 g/kg DM and ME content from 10 to 11 MJ/kg DM.

Availability

Currently bran is much in demand, firstly for the manufacture of fibre-fortified human food, and secondly for inclusion in feeds for horses. This means that in practice little is available for ruminants.

Relative value index   92.4

Feed	**WHEATFEED**	*Medium energy : medium protein*

Description Wheatfeed is a general term applied to the mixture of wheat offal arising from modern flour mills. It contains bran which has not been specifically separated and some more starchy fractions arising from later stages of the milling process. The precise characteristics of wheatfeed depend upon the specification of the grist, the amount of flour being separated (extraction rate) and the actual fractions comprising the wheatfeed.

Physical form Wheatfeed is a mealy, fibrous material.

Bulk density

DM content 880 g/kg

Typical nutritional specification (gram per kg DM except for energy)

ME (MJ/kg DM)	11.0	Crude protein	170
D value	680	Oil (method A)	45
NCD	NA	Oil (method B)	NA
NDF	370	Calcium	1
Crude fibre	80	Phosphorus	10
Starch	300	Magnesium	6
Sugar	90	Salt	1
Ash	50	Potassium	12

Nutritional comments It is worthwhile establishing the specifications of different sources of wheatfeed because of the extent to which different supplies can vary. Crude protein content may range from 160 to 210 g/kg DM, oil (method A) from 40 to 70 g/kg DM, and crude fibre from 40 to 100 g/kg DM. The ME content may vary from 10 to 12 MJ/kg DM and may occasionally be even higher when a lot of starch is present in the mixture. The crude protein is relatively digestible (coefficient 0.75) but is degraded rapidly in the rumen (category A).

Availability Supplies are usually available throughout the year, but demand is normally relatively strong.

Relative value index 94.7

CHAPTER 6

BY-PRODUCTS FROM MALTING, BREWING AND DISTILLING

Barley is the cereal which is malted in significant quantities. The process consists of controlled moistening to germinate the barley grain and activate the enzyme (amylase) which converts starch (the food store of the grain) into sugar (maltose). This change is necessary for the preparation of malt drinks and, most importantly, is a prerequisite to the production of alcohol by fermentation. Yeast is unable to break down starch; it can only ferment sugars.

The stage at which the enzyme in the grain has been effectively activated but the food store has not been significantly depleted by the development of a young seedling is indicated by the appearance of a few small rootlets. At this point, before a shoot appears, the biological process is stopped by kilning (rapid heating in a purpose built oven, a malt kiln). The "malted barley" is dried to about 90 percent dry matter and screened to knock off the small dried rootlets, which are known as *malt culms*.

Prior to malting, the barley grains are thoroughly screened so that husk, fibrous debris and broken grains are removed before germination is initiated. These barley screenings, the malt culms and other malt screenings may be available separately for use as a feed, but increasingly they are pelleted together and offered under the collective name of *malt residual pellets* (*MRPs*).

One of the two major users of malted barley is the brewing industry. The product is ground and mashed, which consists of adding hot water to the ground malt to complete the enzymatic change of starch to maltose, which was started during malting (germination), and to dissolve the sugars which are formed. The sugar solution (sweet wort) is run off to be boiled with hops in preparation for the addition of yeasts, which ferment the sugar to alcohol. The drained and/or strained moist malt residues are the familiar *brewers' grains*.

When the wort is boiled, soluble proteins which were run off with the sugar coagulate and precipitate out. This brown gelatinous material, known as *trub*, is separated from the liquid by centrifugation or filtration and it is usually mixed back into the brewers' grains, marginally increasing the protein content of the latter.

During fermentation of the wort, the added yeast grows and multiplies. At the end of the fermentation it is filtered out of the liquid. Some yeast is retained to prime the next brew, but much of it is available for other uses. Most of the yeast is used to produce yeast extract for human foods or to prime fermentation in the distilling industry, where the yeast is killed after every fermentation. Occasionally, *brewers' yeast* is available as an animal feed, usually in a liquid form, as drying this type of material is a very costly process.

The names and characteristics of livestock feeds arising from the distilling industry can be confusing, due to variations in distilling practices and to differences in the raw materials used. The following is a brief outline of the main processes and products.

There are two distinct types of distillation. *Malt distilling* uses only malted barley. *Grain distilling* traditionally used maize but recently it has changed largely to wheat. In grain distillation a small proportion (12 to 20 percent) of malted barley is used as a source of enzyme to convert the cereal starch to sugars, which are then fermented by yeast. The principles of fermentation and distillation employed by the two processes are the same, but the equipment used is different, as are the names and the specifications of the resultant products.

Hot water is added to screened, milled and cooked cereal and/or milled malt to allow or to complete the conversion of starch to sugars, which in turn are dissolved in the liquid. As in brewing, this is known as mashing. Traditionally, the sugar solution (wort) is then run off, leaving the fibrous cereal residues. These moist cereal residues are the distillers' equivalent to brewers' grains, and are referred to as *draff*. They should be qualified by stating their origin, for example, *maize draff* or *malt draff*.

The wort is cooled and yeast is added to ferment the sugars to alcohol. In some grain distilleries, however, yeast is added to the cooled whole mash (wort plus cereal).

During fermentation of the wort the added yeast multiplies, so that some of the original cereal protein and other nitrogenous compounds are synthesised into yeast protein. When fermentation is complete, distillation is carried out to remove and collect the alcohol which has been produced. The liquid remaining after distillation is known as *pot ale* in a malt distillery and *spent wash* in a grain distillery. In some older distilleries the run-off from the vessel in which mashing took place (the mash tun) was rather crude and the spent wash contained substantial amounts of suspended solids. These were sometimes removed by sedimentation and drainage in porous sacks after distillation, and the solids collected were known as *dreg* or, when dried, as *dreg meal*. Distillation is also carried out when the whole mash is fermented, and with this process the watery 'soup' remaining is known as *stillage*.

From the mid 1960s until quite recently, most distillery by-products were dried before being sold as animal feeds. Draff may be pressed to reduce its moisture content, and if the whole mash is fermented the fibrous fraction in the stillage may be separated by screening and/or centrifugation. The resultant materials are known as *pressed draff* and *press* or *centrifuge cake*. These fibrous portions, dried alone, are known as *distillers' light grains*, and again should be qualified by their origin, for example, *malt distillers' light grains*.

The dry matter contents of pot ale, spent wash or thin stillage (stillage with the suspended solids removed), together with any press liquids are increased from 2 to 5 percent to 35 to 50 percent by evaporation; they are then known as *pot ale syrup* or *spent wash syrup*.

Spent wash and thin stillage are similar materials. When syrups are further dried to moisture contents of less than 100 g/kg, they are known as *dried distillers' solubles*. Frequently the pressed fibrous residues and syrups are combined and dried together to produce *distillers' dark grains* (also known as *distillers' grains with solubles*). Again, these should be qualified by stating their origin, for example *wheat distillers' dark grains*.

On occasions the products from single distilleries or by-product treatment plants are marketed under specific names. Products include, for example, Scotaferm and Scotasol (malt distillers' solubles), and Stimuflav and Vitaferm (types of maize distillers' dark grains).

In the UK, changes in distilling practice and the treatment of the by-products of distilling have resulted in wheat largely replacing maize and dreg, dreg meal or dried solubles being rarely produced. *Wheat distillers' dark grains* are now the most widely available UK product. Maize based products are still available as *U.S. corn distillers' dark grains*.

During the last decade blends of draff and syrup which have not been subjected to the final drying phase have become available. The materials are usually blended in appropriate proportions to give them acceptable handling and storage characteristics. A preservative should be added to give biological stability. These moist concentrate feeds are usually highly cost-effective sources of nutrients, although haulage costs mean that their benefits apply primarily to Scotland and to the North of England. Again, products from individual companies may be available under specific names such as Curne Gold (originally of maize origin but now from wheat) and Hairst Gold (malt origin).

The following tables provide general specifications for commonly available by-products from the malting, brewing and distilling industries. Products from individual companies and by-products which are available only in localised areas have not been described.

| Feed | **BREWERS' GRAINS** | *Medium energy : high protein* |

Description Brewers' grains are the drained residues of a 'mash' following hot water extraction of fermentable sugar from malt. The grains consist mainly of fibrous material and protein from barley.

Physical form The moist, pale to mid brown, milled product varies in consistency from friable to porridge-like, depending on the degree to which the malt is ground, the presence of other materials (adjuncts) added to the mash and the type of enzymic activity during mashing. Contrary to popular belief, consistency is not solely a reflection of the moisture content.

Bulk density 900 to 1000 kg/m^3 varying with fineness of milling and moisture content.

DM content Fresh grains: 220 g/kg, determined by oven drying; 240 g/kg, when corrected for volatile constituents.

Typical nutritional specification (gram per kg DM except for energy)

ME (MJ/kg DM)	11.5	Crude protein	210
D value	600	Oil (method A)	77
NCD	580	Oil (method B)	NA
NDF	580	Calcium	3.5
Crude fibre	170	Phosphorus	5
Starch	60	Magnesium	1.5
Sugar	10	Salt	1
Ash	42	Potassium	0.4

Nutritional comments Brewers' grains are particularly useful for ruminants. Removal of starch leaves a concentrated source of digestible fibre and heat-treated protein. Traditionally, brewers' grains resulted in better performance than their listed nutritive value indicated; work around 1980 demonstrated that, as with other low starch/high protein cereal by-products, energy losses as methane during digestion are less than previously assumed. The currently ascribed ME value is higher and matches more closely production levels achieved. Protein degradability appears to be B. Brewers' grains contain relatively good levels of P, but are low in many other minerals. 'Wet' loads occur much less frequently now and information on the DM content should be provided by the supplier. Due to effluent production, ensiled grains generally have a higher DM content than fresh grains, about 280 g/kg oven DM or 300 g/kg corrected DM.

Availability More brewers' grains are produced during the summer than winter, in contrast to the pattern of demand. Prices are usually lower in summer to encourage purchase and ensilage.

Relative value index 27.9

| **Feed** | **DISTILLERS' DARK GRAINS** | *High energy : high protein* |

Description
Malt products are usually brown. Those from maize are often more golden, while wheat-based products may be quite dark brown. They are all darker in colour than light grains or maize gluten feed because of their syrup content.

Physical form
Products leave the driers as moderately fine meals, but they are usually pelleted subsequently to improve handling and transport. Imported products are usually maize based (e.g. US corn distillers' dark grains) and show some degree of mealiness, due to breakdown during frequent handling and shipment.

Bulk density
600 kg/m^3, varying with physical form and original syrup content.

DM content
900 to 910 g/kg

Typical nutritional specification (gram per kg DM except for energy)

	Malt	*Maize*	*Wheat*		*Malt*	*Maize*	*Wheat*
ME (MJ/kg DM)	12.0	13.5	12.5	Crude protein	260	300	300
D value	600	630	650	Oil (method A)	60	100	60
NCD	NA	NA	NA	Oil (method B)	100	150	130
NDF	420	300	350	Calcium	1	3	3
Crude fibre	140	90	75	Phosphorus	7	10	9
Starch	16	3	Trace	Magnesium	3	4	3
Sugar	18	10	7	Salt	1	2	5
Ash	55	50	50	Potassium	8	11	12

Nutritional comments
Distillers' dark grains are well digested and utilized by ruminants, and are usually very palatable. Much of the starch has been removed so they are likely to reduce rumen pH less than whole cereals, and they are therefore good complementary feeds for use with forages. Total protein content is relatively high, both associated with the fibre and supplied by the syrup. Although potentially readily degradable, much of the protein passes through the rumen quickly and actual degradability appears to be category C.

Availability
Grains are available during most of the year, but they are often traded at a discount price during the summer.

Relative value index
Malt: 113.6; maize: 128.7; wheat: 121.5

| Feed | DISTILLERS' SYRUPS | *High energy : high protein* |

Description

Distillers' syrups are highly palatable, golden brown to dark brown syrups with a sharp, salty taste and malty/cooked yeast smell. *Pot ale syrup (PAS)* is produced by evaporating the liquid remaining after the production of malt spirit. *Spent wash syrup (SWS)* is the liquid residue from the production of grain spirit.

Physical form

Syrups vary from medium to very viscous, depending on the level of fine suspended solids, chemical composition of the syrup, and DM content. Generally PAS is less viscous than SWS at a similar DM content. Some syrups, particularly SWS from wheat, are quite fluid when hot and/or agitated, but when stored without heat or agitation tend to gel. Simple storage and handling systems may require distribution at no more than 200 g DM/kg. The pH is usually 3.5 to 4.5.

Bulk density

1020 to 1200 kg/m^3 depending upon content of DM and dissolved solids.

DM content

PAS: 400 to 500 g/kg.
SWS (maize): 350 to 400 g/kg. SWS (wheat): 250 to 350 g/kg.

Typical nutritional specification (gram per kg DM except for energy)

	PAS	SWS (maize)	SWS (wheat)		PAS	SWS (maize)	SWS (wheat)
ME (MJ/kg DM)	14.5	16	15	Crude protein	360	300	350
D value	850	900	910	Oil (method A)	20	70	30
NCD	NA	NA	NA	Oil (method B)	60	150	90
NDF	6	NA	NA	Calcium	3	2	3
Crude fibre	2	<10	25	Phosphorus	18	15	9
Starch	13	NA	5	Magnesium	6	0	3
Sugar	26	NA	100	Salt	4	2	5
Ash	100	80	60	Potassium	22	15	15

Nutritional comments

These high energy and protein liquids have been incorporated into compound feeds without specialist equipment. Most syrups not incorporated into dark grains are used directly on farms, in home mixes or fed through mixer wagons, troughs or ball feeders. The protein is soluble or in fine suspension and appears readily degraded (A), although the liquid feed passes rapidly through the rumen and some protein may escape degradation. (The degradability in practice may be B). Syrups are useful supplements to improve digestion and utilisation of low protein, fibrous feeds. They contain a useful amount of P but little Ca; the high level of K may be associated with scouring if excess is fed. An intake of 1 to 4 kg daily is a practical, cost-effective recommendation.

Availability

Distillers' syrups are available most of the year, but prices are often less during summer, when demand is lowest. Due to haulage costs, syrups are cheaper in Scotland and Northern England than in the Midlands, Wales and Southern England.

Relative value index

PAS: 71.1, SWS maize: 57.0, SWS wheat: 48.3

Feed	**MALT CULMS AND MALT RESIDUAL PELLETS**
	Medium energy : high protein

Description

Malt culms, the dried rootlets from malting barley, are mid brown or brown/grey in colour. By contrast, the mixture of materials comprising malt residue pellets (MRP) ressembles the colour of barley grain, with the starch from broken grains showing as white flecks.

Physical form

Malt culms originate as a relatively low density meal, but currently if they are available as a separate feed they are often pelleted to improve handling and storage. Malt residues are normally pelleted, forming a fairly dense, hard pellet.

Bulk density

Malt culms: 450 kg/m³. MRPs: 650 to 750 kg/m³.

DM content

900 g/kg

Typical nutritional specification (gram per kg DM except for energy)

	Malt culms	MRP		Malt culms	MRP
ME (MJ/kg DM)	11.0	11.5	Crude protein	270	220
D value	720	680	Oil (method A)	10	22
NCD	NA	NA	Oil (method B)	NA	23
NDF	NA	NA	Calcium	3	2.2
Crude fibre	160	135	Phosphorus	7	6
Starch	6	175	Magnesium	1.5	2
Sugar	165	NA	Salt	1	3
Ash	75	65	Potassium	2	14

Nutritional comments

Both malt culms and the general blend of malting residues have a useful nutritional value and are particularly suited to feed to ruminants. Malt culms fed alone tend to be bitter but when mixed with other feed or as part of malt residual pellets they are accepted readily. The relatively high overall nutritive value and good physical properties of malt residual pellets lend them to intensive beef production. Their energy value however is somewhat less than that of cereal grain and for the best results, to make full use of their protein content, they should be mixed with cereal grains or with other high energy feeds.

Availability

Malting takes place throughout the year and the by-products are therefore also available on a continuous basis. The amounts of both malt culms and malt residual pellets produced are, however, limited and demand may exceed supply.

Relative value index

Malt culms: 107.6, MRPs: 105.8

CHAPTER 7

BY-PRODUCTS FROM THE SUGAR INDUSTRY

The world sugar industry is based upon sugar cane (*Saccharum officinarum* L.), widely grown in the tropics, and sugar beet (*Beta vulgaris* L. var. saccharifera), which is cultivated in temperate climates. Sugars derived from the transformation of cereal starch are, however, growing in importance.

Sugar cane is a grass which reaches around 3 metres in height and 5 to 6 cm in diameter in about eighteen months, when it is ready to harvest. The leaves are removed prior to harvest either by cutting, when they are left to form a mulch, or by burning. The cane is chopped and crushed to allow the sugar to be extracted using water. The fibrous residue remaining after sugar extraction is known as *bagasse* or *megasse*. It is used as a forage feed near sugar factories, but its nutritive value does not justify further processing and transport.

The sugar solution is clarified and filtered. This is followed by evaporation under vacuum and centrifugation, which allows sugar crystals to be removed for further refining. The dark brown viscous liquid remaining, from which no more crystalline sugar can be economically removed, is known as *blackstrap molasses* (ie *cane molasses*).

Harvested sugar beet is topped, tailed and washed before being sliced up into cossettes and the sugar removed by hot water. The extraction of crystalline sugar, and the production of molasses is by similar processes to those used in the cane industry. The fibrous residue, or *beet pulp*, is pressed using heavy rollers to produce a product around 25 percent dry matter which may be made available as a feed in that form, or may be mixed back with the *beet molasses*. In England, molassed pressed pulp is usually dried and distributed as shreds or pellets.

Pressed pulp, either molassed or unmolassed, may be fed fresh or after storage by ensiling. The dried products may be easily stored in a dry place, and can be more easily and economically distributed over wider areas than the moist products.

Molasses is widely used as a feed for its energy content, for its palatability, and for its physical conditioning properties, both in meals and pelleted products and as a base for many liquid products. It is also used as a substrate for industrial fermentation, which leads to the production of another liquid by-product feed, *condensed molasses solubles (CMS)*, which is a less viscous material than molasses. Condensed molasses solubles contain much less sugar than molasses but, as a result of microbial growth, usually have a high protein content.

Most of the UK production of molasses goes either to industrial fermentation or is mixed with sugar beet pulp to produce a range of molassed beet feeds, and the UK animal feed industry is therefore dependent on imports of cane molasses as its source of this feed. In contrast to many raw materials, it is the value and demand for molasses as a fermentation substrate that tends to determine its market price rather than its role as a feed. Further, the supply and demand situation is not simple, as molasses produced in some of the remote equatorial regions only finds its way onto the market if the price is sufficiently attractive. When world molasses prices are low it is cheaper to dispose of the by-product at source.

All dried beet feeds produced in the UK, whether as shreds or pelleted products, are molassed whereas products which are occasionally imported from other European countries may be either molassed or unmolassed.

| Feed | **MOLASSES** | *High energy : low protein* |

Description

Molasses is the sweet smelling, sweet tasting residue remaining after sugar extraction has been completed in either the beet or cane sugar industry.

Physical form

Molasses is a very viscous, dark brown liquid. Inclusion of 2 or 3% can improve the physical characteristics of meals or pellets but 10% and above may cause excessive stickiness. Viscosity varies considerably between different sources, depending on the ratio of dissolved and particulate solids. Supplies available for feeding are usually blended and standardised. Heat is useful for reliable, controlled handling but molasses can be stored and handled cold if large bore (10 to 15 cm) plumbing is used.

Bulk density

1400 kg/m^3

DM content

740 g/kg

Typical nutritional specification (gram per kg DM except for energy)

ME (MJ/kg DM)	12.0	Crude protein	40
D value	780	Oil (method A)	—
NCD	NA	Oil (method B)	—
NDF	—	Calcium	10
Crude fibre	—	Phosphorus	5
Starch	—	Magnesium	3
Sugar	640	Salt	5
Ash	100	Potassium	35

Nutritional comments

Molasses usually increases the palatability of rations, and improves the physical characteristics of meals and pellets by reducing dustiness or increasing the ease with which materials pellet. Energy is mainly from sugars, principally sucrose, which are very rapidly digested. Moderate amounts of molasses appear to stimulate rumen fermentation but an excess leads to a reduction in the proportion of acetate produced, which may decrease the efficiency of feed utilization and reduce the fat content of milk. Excess molasses also often leads to scouring due, in part at least, to the high levels of potassium present. The precise effects of different levels of molasses in a diet depend upon other dietary constituents. Up to 20% inclusion in the total diet is often reported as feasible, but in practice an overall inclusion rate of about 10% appears to be most satisfactory.

Availability

Molasses is usually available throughout the year, and is often sold at a small discount during the summer months.

Relative value index

73.9

| Feed | **SUGAR BEET PULP (MOLASSED)** *High energy : low protein* |

Description   The residues left after the extraction of juice from the topped and tailed roots of sugar beet are mixed with molasses.

Physical form   Molassed beet pulp is a grey/brown material which is available as a dense moist pulp, as dried shreds or as pellets.

Bulk density   Moist pulp: 1000 kg/m^3. Dried pelleted product: 1250 kg/m^3.

DM content   Moist pulp: 250 g/kg. Dried products: 900 g/kg

Typical nutritional specification (gram per kg DM except for energy)

ME (MJ/kg DM)	12.5	Crude protein	110
D value	820	Oil (method A)	5
NCD	NA	Oil (method B)	NA
NDF	300	Calcium	6
Crude fibre	130	Phosphorus	0.8
Starch	—	Magnesium	1.5
Sugar	250	Salt	7.5
Ash	82	Potassium	16

Nutritional comments   The fibrous residues of sugar beet comprise mainly cellulose, which is highly digestible. Thus when fed with an appropriate supplement of degradable protein, beet pulp is an exceptionally suitable feed for ruminants. It is particularly suited to milk production as it helps to maintain optimum rumen conditions which encourages a high acetate : propionate ratio in the VFA produced.

Availability   Beet pulp is available mainly from October to February, following the sugar beet harvest. But in some years, depending on the initial uptake, supplies of the dried product may be available during most of the summer months.

Relative value index   Pressed pulp (250g DM/kg): 28.1
Dried product (900 g DM/kg): 101.0.

CHAPTER 8

BY-PRODUCTS FROM FRUIT AND VEGETABLE PROCESSING

Many thousands of tonnes of fruit and vegetables are prepared or processed for human consumption, worldwide. Internationally the most significant types of processing are grapes for wine or juice, citrus fruits for canning or juice, and olives for preserving. Many of the by-products formed are used locally in the country of origin but some are dried and traded internationally. Although a certain amount of relatively low grade material, such as dried *olive pulp* and *grape pulp*, finds its way to the UK, dried *citrus pulp* is the most important of the imported products. Broadly speaking, when the price is right citrus pulp offers a useful alternative to dried beet pulp.

The number of apples grown in the West and South West of the UK for apple juice and for cider gives rise to significant quantities of *apple pomace*. Additionally, the extraction of pectin from apples and citrus fruit results in the production of *pectin extracted fruit (PEF)*. Cider making is seasonal, but pectin is extracted throughout the year. By-products from both are suited to on-farm use, and they should be handled and stored in a similar manner to brewers' grains or moist beet pulp.

Vegetable processing in the UK results in rejected vegetables, trimmings and by-products being available on occasions. These *vegetable wastes* are usually purchased by livestock producers who are situated fairly locally to the packing centre or processing plant.

Potato tubers are swollen underground stems which store starch. They are grown primarily for human consumption but those surplus to human needs, and the by-products from processing are useful animal feeds.

Manioc, also known as cassava or tapioca, produces roots rich in starch. These are not only used widely as a human food, but many thousands of tonnes are also dried and prepared as an animal feed.

Feed	**APPLE POMACE**	*Medium energy : low protein*

Description

Apples (*Malus sylvestris* Ssp Mitis (Wallr)) are pressed between September and February. The juice is either prepared and packaged for drinking direct, or it is used to make cider. The residues (pomace) contain the core tissues, pressed flesh and skins. The dry matter content varies over the season, being lowest at the beginning and progressively increasing as the apples being processed become older.

Physical form

Apple pomace is a stiff, moist porridge-like material.

Bulk density

DM content

160 to 300 g/kg, varying with season

Typical nutritional specification (gram per kg DM except for energy)

ME (MJ/kg DM)	9.0	Crude protein	60
D value	570	Oil (method A)	35
NCD	NA	Oil (method B)	NA
NDF	500	Calcium	2
Crude fibre	21	Phosphorus	2
Starch	—	Magnesium	0.5
Sugar	160	Salt	1
Ash	30	Potassium	5

Nutritional comments

High levels of pectins may cause digestive disorders in young ruminants but apple pomace can be safely fed to older animals. The product has been fed successfully at up to 20% of the ration, although 10% is a more usual inclusion rate.

Availability

Apples are usually pressed between late September and February and the product is therefore available during this period. Fresh material can be ensiled to extend its period of use.

Relative value index

18.1

Feed	**BRUSSEL SPROUT PACKHOUSE WASTE**
	Medium energy : high protein

Description
There are several different types of waste resulting from a variety of vegetable processing procedures. Brussel sprouts (*Brassica oleracea germifera*) give rise to stripped stems, foliage waste and packhouse waste, the latter consisting of blown sprouts and outer leaves.

Physical form
Loose green material

Bulk density

DM content
150 g/kg

Typical nutritional specification (gram per kg DM except for energy)

ME (MJ/kg DM)	11.1	Crude protein	235
D value	—	Oil (method A)	26
NCD	—	Oil (method B)	—
NDF	—	Calcium	15.5
Crude fibre	139	Phosphorus	3.7
Starch	—	Magnesium	—
Sugar	—	Salt	—
Ash	122	Potassium	—

Nutritional comments
Like all brassica wastes and trimmings, Brussel sprout packhouse waste is a useful source of protein. It has a higher protein content than other green vegetable waste, except perhaps that from cauliflower, and it can be a supplement to or partly substitute for forage. However, because it contains goitrogenic substances (eg SMCO; S- methyl cystine sulphoxide) which can interfere with iodine uptake by the thyroid gland and may cause haemolytic anaemia, it is advisable to offer brussel sprout waste at no more than 15% of the dietary dry matter. Brussel sprout packhouse waste has a much higher calcium content than that of phosphorus, but the importance of this can only be assessed when the overall ration has been formulated.

Availability
Sprouts are harvested between October and March. The most important growing areas are East Anglia, East Midlands and Yorkshire.

Relative value index
17.4

Feed	**CARROTS**	*High energy : low protein*

Description

The carrot (*Dancus carota* Ssp. *sativus* (Hoffm.) Arcang) is a familiar root vegetable in the UK. Sometimes after carrots have been washed in preparation for pre-packing or canning they are rejected on the basis of size, shape or broken roots. These rejected carrots are a clean, wholesome feed but because they are washed they may not keep well. A storage period of 10 to 14 days may be expected in cool weather but this will be much reduced in mild and/or humid weather.

Physical form

Carrots are present as washed, whole and broken roots

Bulk density

DM content

120 g/kg

Typical nutritional specification (gram per kg DM except for energy)

ME (MJ/kg DM)	12.8	Crude protein	90
D value	810	Oil (method A)	15
NCD	NA	Oil (method B)	NA
NDF	NA	Calcium	5.0
Crude fibre	100	Phosphorus	3.0
Starch	110	Magnesium	1.8
Sugar	NA	Salt	2.0
Ash	69	Potassium	NA

Nutritional comments

Carrots are a highly palatable feed.

Availability

Carrots are harvested over a fairly long period from September to February. The vast majority are grown in East Anglia, with some being produced in Yorkshire.

Relative value index

13.5

| Feed | CITRUS PULP | *High energy : low protein* |

Description

When citrus fruits, primarily oranges and grapefruit, are processed for their juice up to 60% of the original fruit remains as peel, rag (inner tissues) and pips. These residues may be used as an animal feed either in the moist form near the processing plant (usually in the tropical and sub-tropical countries of origin) or more often as a dried pelleted product. Calcium (as limestone) or sodium hydroxide is usually added to assist drying. Overall quality is influenced by the exact mixture of fruits being processed and whether or not the seeds are included in the pulp. The dried product has a characteristic citrus aroma which appears readily acceptable to animals.

Physical form

Yellow/brown shredded and ground material is produced, but pellets are most commonly imported into the UK. These are generally of reasonable quality, although some breakdown may take place. Most consignments flow well and can be blown.

Bulk density

700 kg/m^3

DM content

890 g/kg

Typical nutritional specification (gram per kg DM except for energy)

ME (MJ/kg DM)	12.5	Crude protein	72
D value	800	Oil (method A)	25
NCD	NA	Oil (method B)	30
NDF	250	Calcium	14
Crude fibre	130	Phosphorus	2
Starch	Trace	Magnesium	2
Sugar	240	Salt	1
Ash	70	Potassium	11

Nutritional comments

The seeds of citrus contain limonin which is toxic to pigs and poultry, although ruminants do not appear to be affected. A high oil content usually indicates the inclusion of seeds. In general its good palatability and relatively high energy content allow citrus pulp to be used freely in ruminant diets. Dairy cows can be fed 4 to 5 kg per day, but attention must be paid to ensure that overall levels of dietary protein are adequate, and that the supply of minerals and vitamins is balanced.

Availability

Citrus pulp is usually freely available during the winter feeding period provided that it can be offered at a competitive price on the UK market.

Relative value index

95.9

Feed	**MANIOC**	*High energy : low protein*

Description

Manioc (*Manihot esculenta* Crantz), also known as cassava or tapioca, is a large tropical and subtropical shrub which can grown up to 4 metres high. It is grown for its starch-laden tuberous roots, which may be used for humans and animals. When harvested, the roots are usually peeled, ground or sliced and dried naturally in the sun for about two weeks.

Physical form

Manioc is traded as dried chips, ground meals or a pelleted product. The dried root flesh is off-white in colour, usually with some dark brown skin residues. The skin residues may be evident in meal or pellets as well as on the surface of chips. The hard pelleted forms are probably the easiest to handle.

Bulk density

650 to 750 kg/m^3 (good quality pellets will be the most dense).

DM content

880 g/kg

Typical nutritional specification (gram per kg DM except for energy)

ME (MJ/kg DM)	12.8	Crude protein	30
D value	880	Oil (method A)	6
NCD	NA	Oil (method B)	NA
NDF	80	Calcium	2
Crude fibre	40	Phosphorus	1
Starch	680	Magnesium	1
Sugar	40	Salt	1
Ash	55	Potassium	9

Nutritional comments

Clean, well-dried and processed consignments of manioc are primarily sources of starch, and little else. The raw root contains varying amounts of glucosides, particularly linamarin, which may be enzymatically hydrolysed to hydrocyanic (prussic) acid. Well-peeled and dried roots offer the least risk. The Feeding Stuffs Regulations 1988 prohibit the trading of manioc products with greater than 100 mg/kg (at 880 g DM/kg) hydrocyanic acid, and fresh weight standards of no more than 140 g/kg moisture, 50 g/kg crude fibre or 30 g/kg siliceous matter and at least 620 g/kg starch have been set for importation into the EEC. These should ensure well-prepared, soil-free products which can be used at up to 30 or even 40% in concentrates for ruminants. The small amount of protein present is classed as B degradability.

Availability

Thailand, and to a lesser extent Indonesia and China, are major exporting countries but UK imports have fallen during the last few years and currently it is not regularly offered.

Relative value index

92.5

Feed	**PECTIN EXTRACTED FRUIT**		*Medium energy : low protein*

Description When apples and citrus pulp are processed to remove pectin for use in the preparation of other fruit products such as jams and preserves, a moist fruit pulp remains. This pectin extracted fruit (PEF) can be handled and stored like other moist feeds, such as brewers' grains or pressed beet pulp.

Physical form PEF is an off-white/yellowish pulp

Bulk density

DM content 200 g/kg on average, but ranging from 160 to 250 g/kg.

Typical nutritional specification (gram per kg DM except for energy)

ME (MJ/kg DM)	10.0	Crude protein	106
D value	600	Oil (method A)	35
NCD	NA	Oil (method B)	NA
NDF	740	Calcium	NA
Crude fibre	400	Phosphorus	NA
Starch	NA	Magnesium	NA
Sugar	6	Salt	NA
Ash	2	Potassium	NA

Nutritional comments Nutritionally PEF resembles a medium to poor quality forage. The high digestible fibre content means that PEF is particularly suited for feeding to ruminants, but it is a processed product and should always be given in diets which also contain long fibre.

Availability Some PEF is available most of the year, primarily in the South West.

Relative value index 18.4

Feed	**POTATOES**	*High energy : low protein*

Description
The potato (*Solanum tuberosum* L.) is grown for its tubers which make an excellent human food. They may be available for feeding to animals either as discards during sorting and grading or from the release of excessive stocks of stored ware potatoes. The latter will normally be denatured with an edible dye to prevent them from being sold subsequently for human consumption.

Physical form
Discarded or surplus potatoes are presented as whole tubers.

Bulk density

DM content
200 g/kg

Typical nutritional specification (gram per kg DM except for energy)

ME (MJ/kg DM)		13.0	Crude protein	105
D value		880	Oil (method A)	4
NCD		NA	Oil (method B)	NA
NDF		73	Calcium	1.0
Crude fibre		25	Phosphorus	2.2
Starch		562	Magnesium	1.5
Sugar		64	Salt	0.5
Ash		50	Potassium	20

Nutritional comments
Potatoes are a useful energy feed, with a fairly constant composition. Like cereal grains their main energy source is starch, and an excess may therefore lead to acid conditions in the rumen and/or scouring. Badly soiled, rotten and green tubers should be avoided. Dairy cows may successfully be given up to 15% of their dry matter intake as potatoes and beef cattle as much as 40 to 50%. Occasionally when tubers between the size of a hen's egg and a tennis ball have been offered, animals have choked on them. To reduce the risk of choking it is a good general precaution to offer potatoes from the ground.

Availability
Main crop potatoes are typically lifted between July and October in the UK. Sorting and, in some years, release of stored stocks may extend their availability into the following year.

Relative value index
23.1

CHAPTER 9

HIGH TEMPERATURE DRIED FORAGES

Green crop drying, primarily of grasses and legumes, was practised quite widely in the UK between its introduction in the 1930s and the early 1950s. Later, the advent of more efficient driers led to a revival from the mid 1960s to early 1970s. The cost of artificial drying has always been relatively high and currently it is such that, despite the high efficiency of nutrient conservation, little drying takes place in the UK. Home-produced supplies are, however, supplemented by modest imports of dried lucerne from Denmark and the USA.

The digestibility and overall nutritional value of dried forages depend upon the species grown and the stage of growth at which the crop is harvested. For ease of handling and storage, dried forages are usually milled and pelleted. Milling increases the amount of a dried forage that ruminants can consume, largely by increasing the rate at which it passes through the digestive system. The increased rate of passage resulting from milling usually leads to increased loss of energy in the faeces and an overall reduction in digestibility, but other energy losses are reduced so that the net energy content per unit of dry matter consumed is increased. The improvement in overall energy value due to milling is more marked for medium and poor quality forages than for those of high digestibility.

The effect of heat during drying and the increase in rate of passage due to milling improves the nutritive value of the protein fraction of dried forages given to ruminants, compared to that of fresh or ensiled forages. The extent to which the forage protein is degraded in the rumen is reduced by drying, thus increasing the flow of feed protein to the small intestine. Excessive heat, however, is damaging and will result in a substantial reduction in dry matter digestibility, particularly the digestibility of the protein fraction.

Historically, dried forages have been used in poultry diets as a source of beta carotene, a precursor of vitamin A. For this role, the products were traded on the basis of beta carotene and protein contents. In contrast, for ruminants digestibility or energy value is the most important characteristic of a dried forage. The protein content is also important but less so than the energy value. A link has recently been demonstrated between beta carotene supply and fertility in dairy cows which, together with the capability of dried forages, particularly legumes, to increase rumen buffering capacity to resist extremely acid conditions makes the inclusion of modest levels of dried forages in ruminant rations worth considering, particularly for dairy cows. Some measure of digestibility or fibre content to allow an estimate of metabolisable energy content should be determined, so that the use of low energy products in the diets of ruminants with high productive potential can be avoided.

Some producers of dried forages have adopted the star grading system to categorise their products. In practice the star grading is assessed by determining the fibre content of the material but the system is intended to indicate the metabolisable energy content of products. Thus 4* denotes an energy content of 10 MJ ME/kg DM, 3* denotes 9 MJ ME/kg DM and 2* denotes 8.5 MJ ME/kg DM. The different star grades are produced at different protein contents, described commercially in terms of percent crude protein in the fresh weight. Thus, a 14% CP dried grass will contain about 15.5 percent crude protein in the dry matter.

| Feed | **GRASS (DRIED)** | *Low/medium energy : medium protein* |

Description

The high temperature drying of grass, probably predominantly ryegrass (*Lolium* species), is still practised by a few producers in the UK. Different varieties are grown to give a spread of initial heading dates in the spring, and subsequently a series of cuts throughout the growing season. Crops are often batched and traded on the basis of their protein content and star (fibre) rating.

Physical form

Dried grass is usually milled and pelleted. The production units remaining in operation are based on continuously operated high temperature driers, taking the chopped grass for milling and pelleting immediately after drying.

Bulk density

Meal: 200 to 300 kg/m^3; pellets 575 to 675 kg/m^3

DM content

900 g/kg

Typical nutritional specification (gram per kg DM except for energy)

	14%CP, 3*	16%CP, 4*		14%CP, 3*	16%CP, 4*
ME (MJ/kg DM)	9.0	10.0	Crude protein	155	178
D value	550	680	Oil (method A)	35	40
NCD	670	815	Oil (method B)	NA	NA
NDF	560	510	Calcium	90	80
Crude fibre	250	200	Phosphorus	30	35
Starch	60	50	Magnesium	17	16
Sugar	100	140	Salt	6	7
Ash	120	100	Potassium	21	23

Nutritional comments

Dried grass contains useful levels of protein and beta carotene, although these are usually not as high as for legumes. The heat applied during drying, and the effect of milling means that some of the protein escapes degradation in the rumen and contributes directly to the supply of amino acids in the small intestine. Dried grass is usually classified as having a B degradability but with some drying conditions and fine milling it may fall into class C. Milling forages increases voluntary intake but results in the forages being digested more like a concentrate. High levels of milled forages can reduce milk fat content, but dried forage supplements usually have less of a dramatic effect on milk fat than do similar amounts of cereal grains or other starchy feeds.

Availability

Dried grass is not produced in large quantities, but supplies are available most years.

Relative value index

14%CP,3*: 80.9, 16%CP,4*: 90.5

Feed	**LUCERNE (DRIED)**	*Low⁺ energy : medium protein*

Feed   **LUCERNE (DRIED)**   *Low⁺ energy : medium protein*

Description Lucerne (*Medicago sativa* L.), commonly known in the USA as alfalfa, is a deep-rooted, perennial, herbaceous legume with trifoliate leaves and purple flowers. It has never been a popular crop in the UK, but small amounts are grown for fresh use and for drying. Most of the leaf portion may be lost during haymaking, and harvesting before full flower (early bloom) appears to reduce losses and to maximise the yield of productive material.

Physical form Dried lucerne is usually milled and pelleted. The pellets can be quite hard but brittle, and when they break down the product can become very dusty because of the way in which the leaf fraction shatters to a fine powder when dry. Lucerne is often pelleted with 5 to 10% molasses, in an attempt to reduce dustiness.

Bulk density 650 to 700 kg/m³

DM content 900 g/kg

		17%CP,2*		*17%CP,2**
Typical	ME (MJ/kg DM)	8.5	Crude protein	190
nutritional	D value	550	Oil (method A)	32
specification	NCD	600	Oil (method B)	NA
(gram per kg	NDF	480	Calcium	14
DM except for	Crude fibre	270	Phosphorus	3
energy)	Starch	12	Magnesium	2
	Sugar	55	Salt	2
	Ash	11	Potassium	20

Nutritional comments Traditionally dried lucerne has been valued for its protein and β carotene contents, and it has been used primarily in diets for pigs and poultry. The degradability of the protein (B) means that it is particularly useful to ruminants and the role of β carotene in the fertility of dairy cows is important. The ME content of lucerne is low compared to that of typical dried grass, but in common with other legumes lucerne is eaten in higher quantities than comparable grasses. Substantial evidence indicates that the ME is used more efficiently than that from grass and many other feeds. The ratio of cell contents to fibre is higher than in grasses and the high Ca content is often a small bonus to the overall good nutritional value of dried lucerne.

Availability Dried lucerne is not always available and is only imported when it is cost-effective compared to alternative feeds.

Relative value index 81.1

⁺ See Nutritional Comments for clarification

CHAPTER 10

OILSEEDS AND OILSEED RESIDUES

Several crops are important for the oil content of their seeds. Globally, the most widespread is the soya bean followed by cotton, groundnut, sunflower and rapeseed, with others such as palm kernel, coconut, linseed, sesame and safflower being less important. Oilseed rape and, to some extent, sunflowers are being increasingly grown in Europe.

During processing some seeds may have part of their outer, fibrous layers removed (dehulling or decortication) before the actual removal of oil, which may be achieved simply by crushing (expeller) or by crushing followed by the use of chemical solvents (extraction). The outer fibrous material may or may not be used as a livestock feed. For example, soya bean hulls are available either as a separate feed or they may be blended back into the meal which remains after the removal of oil. In contrast, the outer fibrous layer from coconuts is used to manufacture coconut matting rather than as a livestock feed. The residues remaining after removal of the oil contain most of the fibrous carbohydrate and protein fractions present in the original seeds. These residues form the group of feeds known as oilseed meals.

Oilseed meals have broadly similar nutritional characteristics and to some extent they are interchangeable. Their nutritive value varies with the amount and digestibility of the carbohydrate fraction, the level and type of the protein present and the content of residual oil. The carbohydrate fraction comprises different proportions of fibre, starch and sugar, which influences the digestibility and therefore the energy value of the meal. In general, the most fibrous materials are the least digestible.

Dehulling or decortication removes some of the most indigestible fibre and improves the efficiency of oil removal. The digestibility of the fibrous residue is increased, but the residual oil content may be reduced. The metabolisable energy content of extracted, dehulled soya bean meal, which contains about 40 g/kg DM crude fibre, is approximately 13.3 MJ/kg DM, despite the oil content being little over 10 g/kg DM. In contrast, extracted, partly decorticated sunflower seed meal may have a crude fibre content as high as 260 g/kg DM and, with an oil content of only 20 g/kg DM, the resulting energy content for ruminants is barely 9.0 MJ ME/kg DM. Oil has a high energy content, which raises the metabolisable energy content of feeds high in oil, but in some circumstances an excess of free, unsaturated oil can have an adverse effect on the digestion of fibre in the rumen.

As might be expected, expeller materials contain more oil than residues from extraction. Expeller, decorticated sunflower seed meal generally has a metabolisable energy content of 12 MJ/kg DM, with a typical crude fibre content of 135 g/kg DM (12 percent in the fresh material) and a residual oil content of 145 g/kg DM (13 percent in the fresh material).

Traditionally, oilseed meals have been described for trading purposes by the combined content of oil and protein in their fresh weights. This is referred to at different times as "O and A" (oil and albumen) or "profat". Using this system of description, a "44" soya bean meal would typically contain 42.5 percent crude protein and 1.5 percent oil in its fresh weight (475 g and 17 g/kg DM respectively). "40/42" as applied to cottonseed meal means the combined value of protein and oil should lie between 40 and 42 percent in the fresh weight.

Some qualification of the fibre content, particularly in the case of soya bean meal, is sometimes linked with the trade protein and oil nomenclature. Thus, "44/7" indicates a maximum fibre content of 7 percent in the fresh weight (79 g/kg DM), "44/11" indicates a maximum crude fibre content of 11 percent in the fresh weight, whilst "44/0" indicates that the 44 specification will be met, not in the absence of fibre but without any guarantees regarding fibre content. These descriptions are still used in trading, even though the feeding stuffs legislation requires a statutory statement showing the contents of protein, fibre and oil for expeller products, and protein and fibre for extracted products. In practice, contractual obligations and the legislative requirements to provide specific analytical information are dealt with quite separately.

Many of the oilseeds contain antinutritive substances. Some, like the trypsin inhibitor found in soya beans, are inactivated by the heat produced during processing, but others such as the glucosinolates of rapeseed are more persistent and remain active in the resultant meals. Account must be taken of the latter type of antinutritive factor when deciding the levels at which the different oilseed meals may be used.

Rapeseed contains two types of antinutritive substances: erucic acid which is found in the oil, and glucosinolates which are found in the cell wall structure. Plant breeding programmes have been carried out to produce varieties of oilseed rape which have very low levels of these substances. Varieties with low levels of erucic acid in the seed are known as 'single low' varieties and are already widely grown commercially. Varieties low in both erucic acid and glucosinolates are known as 'double low' varieties and commercially viable examples are now becoming available. EEC legislation defines the level of glucosinolates which constitute 'low' meals, and only these will attract growers' subsidies after 1991. Currently, 35 µmol/ kg DM is the defined standard but the target is not more than 20 µmol/kg DM.

Many of the oilseeds are grown extensively in tropical and sub-tropical climates, which means that the products are frequently stored under warm, moist conditions. In such situations they are susceptible to moulding, and in certain circumstances fungal poisons (mycotoxins) may be produced. Mycotoxins, of which the aflatoxins are an important group, are undesirable substances which may cause pathological and physiological changes in man and animals. Raw materials should be tested for the presence of mycotoxins whenever there has been a risk of them forming.

The Feeding Stuffs Regulations, 1988, make it illegal for anyone to sell or to possess with a view to sell most straights containing aflatoxin B_1 at more than 0.05 mg/kg (adjusted to 12 percent moisture). Complete and complementary feeds for cattle, sheep and goats must also contain no more than 0.05 mg/kg aflatoxin B_1. Further, complete and complementary feeds intended for dairy cows, calves, lambs or goat kids must contain no more than 0.01 mg/kg aflatoxin B_1 (adjusted to 12 percent moisture).

From 3 December 1988, "Groundnut, copra, palm-kernal, cotton seed, babassu, maize and products derived from the processing thereof" intended solely for use by manufacturers of feedstuffs who appear on the national list can, under specific conditions, be traded with levels of aflatoxin B_1 up to 0.2 mg/kg (adjusted to 12 percent moisture). Products with levels between 0.05 and 0.2 mg/kg (at 12 percent moisture) must be accompanied at all times by a document stating the actual level.

There is evidence available to suggest that the oil in oilseeds is most useful, particularly for ruminants, if it remains associated with the rest of the seed. It appears that oil in this form is less freely released in the rumen and thus interferes less with fibre digestion. Thus, increasingly whole oilseeds are being considered as feeds. Soya beans are available processed in a variety of ways, the most important of which are extrusion, micronisation or wet cooking under pressure. Whole palm kernels are also available and experimental work is in progress to determine the most appropriate methods of processing oilseed rape.

The following tables cover whole soya beans and a representative range of oilseed residues, produced by expeller and by extraction processes.

Feed	**COPRA EXPELLER PRODUCTS**	*High energy : high protein*

Description Copra is the dried flesh of the coconut (*Cocos nucifera* L.), which grows in most of the world's equitorial regions. The DM contains between 60 and 70% oil, which is usually removed by an expeller process for use in human foods and for quality soap manufacture. The residues remaining are pale to mid-brown in colour.

Physical form The expeller residues are available in a variety of forms including meals, pellets, cakes and flakes, which are all slightly tacky to touch, due to the residual oil. They are not dusty.

Bulk density 400 to 600 kg/m^3, depending upon whether pelleted or not.

DM content 900 g/kg

Typical nutritional specification (gram per kg DM except for energy)

ME (MJ/kg DM)	13.0	Crude protein	220
D value	650	Oil (method A)	75
NCD	NA	Oil (method B)	NA
NDF	520	Calcium	1.8
Crude fibre	125	Phosphorus	6.5
Starch	NA	Magnesium	3.0
Sugar	140	Salt	5.0
Ash	65	Potassium	15.0

Nutritional comments Ruminants appear to find copra residues very palatable, the sugar content imparting sweetness. As they are eaten very readily, introduction into home mixed rations where selection is possible should be done gradually. A substantial amount of energy is from digestible fibre, although the oil, which is mainly saturated, also makes a significant contribution. The use of copra residues tends to result in firm butter and in hard white fat in beef cattle. Protein degradability appears to be at the lower end of category B, but the protein contains only moderate amounts of the amino acids which commonly limit production. Copra residues are generally free from undesirable substances, but freshness should be checked, as rancidity may result in diarrhoea.

Availability Some copra is processed in the UK and supplies are available most of the year.

Relative value index 116.5

Feed	**COTTONSEED CAKE**	*Low/medium energy : high protein*

Description Cotton plants (*Gossypium* species) are grown extensively in China, USA, USSR and India. A very fibrous seed remains when the cotton, lint fibres and the linters have been removed from the fruit. Oil may be removed from the seed by hydraulic press expeller or by extraction with or without decortication. Traditionally undecorticated cake from black seeds is known as 'Egyptian cotton cake' and undecorticated cake from white seeds as 'Bombay cotton cake'. Cotton cakes are usually brown in colour and slightly oily to the touch.

Physical form Cottonseed cake is a mixture of irregular pieces of cake and meal which are often quite fibrous and fluffy. Cotton cake does not run easily in all automated feeding systems, but is a traditional favourite in home mixes and purchased coarse mixes.

Bulk density 500 to 650 kg/m^3

DM content 900 g/kg

Typical nutritional specification (gram per kg DM except for energy)

Partly decorticated cottonseed expeller (40/42)

ME (MJ/kg DM)	10.0	Crude protein	370
D value	650	Oil (method A)	70
NCD	745	Oil (method B)	75
NDF	320	Calcium	2
Crude fibre	170	Phosphorus	8
Starch	13	Magnesium	5
Sugar	68	Salt	1.5
Ash	57	Potassium	17

Nutritional comments Cotton seeds contain an antinutritive substance 'Gossypol' . This biological antioxidant may reduce appetite, inhibit digestion and cause constipation. Cotton derivatives may also contain aflatoxins. Both gossypol and aflatoxins are listed in the Feeding Stuffs Regulations; a maximum of 1200 mg/kg gossypol and 0.05 mg/kg aflatoxin B_1 are allowed at 88% DM. Gossypol is of little significance to mature ruminants. Slight reductions in appetite with high levels of cotton seed use can be countered by adding ferrous sulphate to the diet. Inclusion levels in concentrate mixes of up to 20%, and possibly higher, are quite acceptable. The product has been used to reduce the laxative effect of high levels of molasses. Overall energy and protein levels depend on the extent of decortication and oil removal. Protein degradability is usually considered category B. Partly-decorticated 40/42 cottonseed expeller, often of Chinese origin, is most commonly available in the UK.

Availability Cotton cake is available most of the year, but is more frequently offered for sale from September to March.

Relative value index 111.2

Feed	**GROUNDNUT CAKE**	*High energy : high protein*

Description Groundnuts (Peanuts or Monkey nuts; *Arachis hypogea* L) are grown in many tropical and subtropical countries, in particular India, China and USA. The whole pod may be crushed for oil, but more often the fibrous hulls are removed by decortication and extraction or expeller processes used to extract the oil.

Physical form Groundnut residues are presented as irregular pieces of brown/dark brown cake or occasionally pellets.

Bulk density 600 to 700 kg/m^3

DM content 900 g/kg

Typical nutritional specification (gram per kg DM except for energy)

Decorticated groundnut cake

	Extr.	Exp.		Extr.	Exp.
ME (MJ/kg DM)	12.5	13.8	Crude protein	550	510
D value	750	770	Oil (method A)	12	70
NCD	NA	NA	Oil (method B)	NA	NA
NDF	NA	180	Calcium	1.8	2
Crude fibre	90	80	Phosphorus	6.5	6
Starch	NA	60	Magnesium	3.5	3
Sugar	NA	90	Salt	1	1
Ash	60	65	Potassium	13	13

Nutritional comments Groundnuts and their derivatives are particularly susceptible to contamination by aflatoxins. Importation of products was banned in 1981 because of national concern over aflatoxin levels in milk. The ban has now been lifted but all imports must comply with the specified maximum levels. Groundnuts and their derivatives are one of six named groups of materials with specific rules, which came into effect in December 1988, relating to their contents of aflatoxin B. Aflatoxin-free groundnut residues are practical alternatives to soya bean meals. The protein is well balanced but more rapidly degraded (category A) than that of soya. At similar oil contents the energy value is not quite as high as that of soya bean meal. Dietary levels up to 20% in concentrate mixes are acceptable.

Availability Reaction to the concern in 1980/81 over aflatoxin levels means that in practice very little is now imported and groundnut meals are not often offered in the UK. From 3 December 1988 the new legislation, which allows trade to listed manufacturers of products containing 0.2 mg/kg aflatoxin (at 88% DM), may increase the amount coming into Europe and the UK.

Relative value index Extracted: 148.5; Expeller: 153.4

| Feed | **LINSEED MEAL** | *High energy : high protein* |

Description

Linseed (*Linum usitatissimum* L) or flax has been grown for centuries to produce linen but in recent years its oil, which is used in the manufacture of linoleum, paints, printers inks and soaps has been more important. Requirements for linseed oil are declining now but oil is still produced either by extraction or by an expeller process. Linseed expeller is the type of meal most likely to be available in the UK.

Physical form

Linseed meal is available as fairly coarse, irregular sized pieces of cake or extruded lozenges.

Bulk density

650 to 700 kg/m^3

DM content

890 g/kg

Typical nutritional specification (gram per kg DM except for energy)

Linseed Expeller

ME (MJ/kg DM)	13.0	Crude protein	350
D value	750	Oil (method A)	80
NCD	855	Oil (method B)	NA
NDF	250	Calcium	4.3
Crude fibre	100	Phosphorus	8.5
Starch	—	Magnesium	5.2
Sugar	85	Salt	1
Ash	60	Potassium	11.5

Nutritional comments

Linseed meals have a high ME value due to the oil left by the expeller process, and because ruminants can digest the mucilage of linseed very effectively. The high ME is accompanied by a relatively high protein content of moderate degradability (category B). The protein is digestible, although levels of limiting amino acids are not particularly high. Linseed may contain the glucoside linamarin which, if acted upon under certain conditions by the enzyme linase, produces prussic acid. The high temperatures reached during normal processing inactivate the linase and prevent the release of prussic acid, making linseed meal a safe and practical feed. Linseed meal has a laxative effect when offered in large amounts, but up to 20% of the concentrate part of the ration for adult ruminants (slightly less for young stock) seems to be quite acceptable. Linseed meal is often given to produce a good 'bloom' on the coat of animals.

Availability

Linseed meal is usually available throughout the year.

Relative value index

129.0

| Feed | **PALM KERNEL MEAL** | *Medium/high energy : high protein* |

Description — The African Oil Palm (*Elaeis guineensis* Jacq.) is grown mainly in equitorial Asia and West Africa. Palm oil, which is used in soap and food manufacture, is removed from the outer, fleshy skin of the fruit. Palm kernel oil is removed separately by extraction or expeller processes from kernels released from the nut after it has been cracked. Some seeds (nuts) are imported whole for cracking and expelling in the UK. The meal has a characteristic mild, soapy aroma.

Physical form — Palm kernel is a dry, gritty meal, pale brown/cream in colour.

Bulk density — 450 to 600 kg/m^3

DM content — 900 g/kg

Typical nutritional specification (gram per kg DM except for energy)

	Exp.	Extr.		Exp.	Extr.
ME (MJ/kg DM)	12.8	11.5	Crude protein	200	210
D value	750	720	Oil (method A)	70	11
NCD	NA	444	Oil (method B)	NA	NA
NDF	NA	NA	Calcium	2.5	3
Crude fibre	160	17	Phosphorus	5.8	6
Starch	20	20	Magnesium	3.0	3
Sugar	40	40	Salt	2.5	2
Ash	41	42	Potassium	6	6

Nutritional comments — Palm kernel meal is a safe feed, not known to contain anti-nutritive substances. Alone it is not particularly palatable, but in mixes or sweetened with molasses, it is quite acceptable. The meal is a useful source of energy and protein for all mature ruminants, the residual oil content contributing to firm butter or carcase fat. The protein, only just present in sufficient quantities to be termed 'high', is usually categorised B degradability. Levels up to 20% in the diet of adult cattle are acceptable, but inclusion rates are usually 10 to 15%. The non-structural carbohydrate in palm kernel and its derivatives comprises mainly mannans, which belong to the non-sugar group (hexosans) which contains starch and cellulose. The mannans are not, however, removed during techniques to measure sugars or starch, nor are they digested by cellulase. Consequently, when products are subjected to an NCD determination, values are low in relation to those found *in vivo* or by *in vitro* rumen fluid techniques. This has prompted reassessment of enzyme preparations to predict the nutritive value of some feeds.

Availability — Some supplies are available throughout the year.

Relative value index — Expeller: 112.9; Extracted: 104.7

Feed	**RAPESEED MEAL**	*Medium energy : high protein*

Description   The amount of oilseed rape (*Brassica napus* L & B rapa (*campestris*) L) grown has increased markedly in recent years, particularly in Europe. Oil is most commonly removed by extraction to produce a dark brown or black/yellow meal, usually with a burnt cabbage aroma.

Physical form   The friable meal, which is occasionally processed into pellets, is slightly oily to the touch.

Bulk density   500 to 600 kg/m^3

DM content   890 g/kg

Typical nutritional specification (gram per kg DM except for energy)

Extracted rapeseed meal

ME (MJ/kg DM)	11.5	Crude protein	420
D value	700	Oil (method A)	25
NCD	766	Oil (method B)	30
NDF	280	Calcium	7.5
Crude fibre	120	Phosphorus	12
Starch	60	Magnesium	5
Sugar	100	Salt	1
Ash	70	Potassium	12

Nutritional comments   From 1991, production of varieties low in both erucic acid and glucosinolates (double low) will be encouraged within the EEC, by the introduction of selective financial support for seed meeting the specified maximum content of glucosinolates. A dietary inclusion rate of about 10% is usually advocated for meal from single low varieties, but typically inclusion rates are about 5%. Excessive amounts are thought to be associated with symptoms of iodine deficiency and enlarged thyroid glands. Where appropriate nutritionally, higher levels of inclusion are possible for meal from double low varieties. Rapeseed meal fed alone is unpalatable but it is quite acceptable to livestock in mixes, at the above levels. Rapeseed meal is a practical and usually cost-effective alternative to soya bean meal for ruminants, provided allowance is made for the lower energy and protein contents. Relatively high levels of phytic acid may reduce the availability of minerals, particularly phosphorus for pigs and poultry.

Availability   Currently meal from UK single low varieties is freely available. Imported meal from double low varieties is often offered for sale.

Relative value index   125.9

Feed	**SAFFLOWER AND SESAME MEAL**

Medium/high energy : high protein

Description

Safflower or false saffron (*Carthamus tinctorius* L) is a member of the thistle family. It is a very old oilseed crop grown mainly in India and the USA, although production is declining. Sesame (*Sesamum indicum* L., *S. orientale* L.) is grown in parts of Asia, the Mediterranean and South America. The seeds of both plants are crushed for oil, mainly by the expeller process but occasionally extraction is used.

Physical form

Safflower and sesame residues are produced as cake and meal.

Bulk density

DM content

900 g/kg

Typical nutritional specification (gram per kg DM except for energy)

	Safflower exp.		Sesame		Safflower exp.		Sesame
	Undec.	Decort.	exp.		Undec.	Decort.	exp.
ME (MJ/kg DM)	8.5	12.0	12.9	Crude protein	250	450	470
D value	NA	NA	700	Oil (method A)	80	100	80
NCD	NA	NA	NA	Oil (method B)	NA	NA	NA
NDF	NA	NA	NA	Calcium	2	4	23
Crude fibre	300	150	70	Phosphorus	6	10	12
Starch	NA	NA	NA	Magnesium	2	4	6
Sugar	NA	NA	NA	Salt	NA	NA	1
Ash	50	80	110	Potassium	9	9	12

Nutritional comments

Safflower seed meal does not appear to contain any antinutritive substances, but when undecorticated it is very fibrous and not particularly palatable. It will, however, be accepted in mixtures. The protein is very digestible in both decorticated and undecorticated products, suggesting degradability class A.

Sesame hulls contain oxalic and phytic acids which make the meal bitter and bind Ca,P and other minerals. As with other expeller meals, the relatively high level of residual oil will, if given in excess, lead to soft and tainted fats. The oil is susceptible to rancidity which increases demand for vitamin E. The meal is relatively high in methionine, cystine and tryptophan and relatively low in lysine, which complements soya bean meal. The protein is digestible and considered category B degradability. Maximum levels of 3 kg/head/day for dairy cows or 15% in the diet of beef cattle appear acceptable.

Availability

Safflower seed meal is rarely offered, whereas sesame seed meal is occasionally available.

Relative value index

Safflower seed meal, expeller, undecorticated: 87.6
decorticated: 134.1
Sesame seed meal, expeller: 142.7

Feed	**SHEA NUT MEAL AND ILLIPE MEAL**

Low energy : medium protein

Description
Shea nut (*Butryospermum paradoxum* (Gaertn.f.) Hepper Ssp. parkii (G. Don)), Illipe or mee (*Madhuca longifolia* (Koening) Maebr., (*Bassia longifolia* L.) and Mowra (*Madhuca indica* J.F. Gmel. also *Bassia latifolia* Roxb.) not only have more than one name for the same plant but, in practice, are often confused with each other. They are all trees grown in Southern Asia for the edible oil from their fleshy seeds. The oil is usually removed by the expeller method. The use of illipe and its derivatives as animal feeds is prohibited in the UK because of their high content of antinutritive substances.

Physical form
These products are cakes or meals.

Bulk density

DM content
900 g/kg

Typical nutritional specification (gram per kg DM except for energy)

Shea nut expeller

ME (MJ/kg DM)	5.0	Crude protein	130
D value	300	Oil (method A)	110
NCD	NA	Oil (method B)	NA
NDF	500	Calcium	3
Crude fibre	100	Phosphorus	2
Starch	20	Magnesium	2
Sugar	120	Salt	2
Ash	70	Potassium	20

Nutritional comments
These oil cakes contain differing amounts of saponin, a toxic substance which damages the mucosal lining of the digestive tract and causes haemolysis of blood. Detoxification is possible by heat treatment but this is barely economic because of the low digestibility and therefore low nutritive value. Between 80 and 90% of the protein in shea nut meals is undegradable in the rumen, and also undigestible. Illipe products are banned from use in the EEC due to their high content of saponins, and shea nut meal is essentially only a "filler" which is best avoided when buying for home mixing and feeding directly on-farm.

Availability
Shea nut meal is occasionally available.

Relative value index
49.7

Feed	**SOYA BEANS (WHOLE PROCESSED)** *High energy : high protein*

Description

The soya bean (*Glycine max* L.) is a hairy legume growing up to about 1 metre high in warm climates. The seeds are borne in typical pods. The raw beans contain anti- nutritional factors like a trypsin inhibitor and haemagglutinins, which must be inactivated before the beans are offered to pigs or poultry. These factors are, however, of little concern to ruminants. Heat processes like micronisation and extrusion which are employed reduce protein degradability in the rumen and possibly reduce the likelihood of intracellular oil being released to interfere with fibre digestion in the rumen.

Physical form

Products normally available are golden or golden brown, granular or flaky meals with a slightly oily touch. They pour and mix reasonably well and, because of their oil content, are not dusty, and can counter dustiness in other feed ingredients.

Bulk density

550 to 600 kg/m³

DM content

890 g/kg, but usually listed as 900 g/kg

Typical nutritional specification (gram per kg DM except for energy)

ME (MJ/kg DM)	15.5	Crude protein	410
D value	700	Oil (method A)	200
NCD	NA	Oil (method B)	NA
NDF	95	Calcium	2.8
Crude fibre	45	Phosphorus	6.0
Starch	20	Magnesium	2.3
Sugar	80	Salt	0.6
Ash	54	Potassium	21

Nutritional comments

Processed whole soya beans are particularly useful when the ration requires additional energy and protein. Correct heat treatment reduces protein degradability with little depression in digestibility. The fact that the oil remains associated with other bean tissues seems to aid passage through the rumen without adverse effects on fibre digestion. Heat also inactivates the various antinutritive substances. When the price is competitive, whole soya beans are particularly useful for young fast-growing animals and cows of high dairy merit. Levels up to 15% of the total dietary dry matter can be used, although this is unlikely in practice. Their most useful future role may be as a constituent in concentrates designed to be offered in limited amounts to maximise forage intake.

Availability

Processed, whole soyabeans are generally available throughout the year.

Relative value index

153.1

| Feed | **SOYA BEAN MEAL** | *High energy : high protein* |

Description

Soya bean meal comprises the residues remaining after the removal of oil from soyabeans. The beans are dehulled before oil is expelled or extracted, the product from the latter being more commonly available in the UK. The composition of the meal varies according to the process used and the amount of hulls blended back. Material is usually referred to by the content of protein *and* oil on a fresh weight basis i.e. soya bean meal 44 contains 42 to 32% CP and 1 to 2% oil. Further qualification such as 44/7 implies a maximum CF content of 7%.

Physical form

Soya bean meal is most often available as a pale, straw coloured, slightly gritty meal, although occasionally some supplies are pelleted.

Bulk density

500 to 600 kg/m^3

DM content

890 g/kg, but usually listed as 900 g/kg

Typical nutritional specification (gram per kg DM except for energy)

	Extracted (44)	Extracted (48)	Exp. (49)		Extracted (44)	Extracted (48)	Exp. (49)
ME (MJ/kg DM)	13.0	13.3	13.5	Crude protein	470	520	480
D value	800	810	800	Oil (method A)	15	10	65
NCD	902	920	910	Oil (method B)	NA	NA	NA
NDF	180	130	120	Calcium	3	3	2
Crude fibre	90	60	55	Phosphorus	7	7	8
Starch	10	10	10	Magnesium	3	3	3
Sugar	80	120	100	Salt	1	1	1
Ash	70	60	63	Potassium	24	25	10

Nutritional comments

Soya bean meal is the most widely used supplementary source of protein worldwide. It combines a high energy value (greater than acknowledged in UK feed tables until recently) with an excellent level of good quality protein. The trypsin inhibitor, is inactivated by heat treatment during processing. Providing heating is not excessive protein damage is minimal. For ruminants degradability is in class B and digestibility is in excess of 0.85.

Availability

Soya bean meal is imported throughout the year, but forward contracting during late summer often allows purchase at the lowest prices.

Relative value index

Soya bean meal type 44/7 has been assigned a value of 145 which, together with the value of 100 assigned to feed barley has been used to calculate the 'relative value index' for all the other feeds described.
Soya bean meal (48) extracted: 150.7.

| Feed | **SUNFLOWER SEED MEAL** | *Low/medium energy : high protein* |

Description Sunflower (*Helianthus annus* L) is a major world crop. The main producers are USSR, USA and Argentina but the area grown in Europe is increasing, particularly in France. The oil may be extracted or expelled but the most common meal in the UK is 'Extracted, partly decorticated', described as 30/35, which is equivalent to 330 to 390 g CP/kg DM.

Physical form Sunflower seed meal is usually presented as grey or off white pellets which may break down. Pieces of the characteristically grey and white striped seed case are often visible.

Bulk density 500 to 600 kg/m^3

DM content 900 g/kg

Typical nutritional specification (gram per kg DM except for energy)

Extracted, partly decorticated sunflower seed meal

	Little hull removed	Substantial hull removed		Little hull removed	Substantial hull removed
ME (MJ/kg DM)	9.0	10.5	Crude protein	320	420
D value	620	670	Oil (method A)	20	20
NCD	NA	635	Oil (method B)	NA	NA
NDF	400	330	Calcium	4.5	4.1
Crude fibre	260	210	Phosphorus	11.0	13.0
Starch	14	15	Magnesium	8.0	8.0
Sugar	60	65	Salt	1.0	1.0
Ash	80	70	Potassium	17.0	16.5

Nutritional There appear to be no anti-nutritive substances in these palatable meals, which can be used freely within the limitations of a balanced diet: up to 20% inclusion is quite acceptable. The overall nutritive value depends upon the proportion of hulls (degree of decortication and blending back) and method of oil removal. A relatively high fibre content and modest energy value often limit use. Expeller products have higher energy values than extracted products due to the residual oil content. This can be as high as 16% in the DM, giving an ME value of about 13 MJ/kg DM. Sunflower meals have a relatively high content of sulphur-containing amino acids and protein degradability is usually rated category B. Freshness, particularly of expeller products, is important as the oil may go rancid during extended storage. The fibre in sunflower meal, particularly the hulls, may be rather harsh to the mouth of young stock.

Availability Limited amounts of meals are usually available throughout the year, but they are most frequently offered from September to March.

Relative value index Extracted partly dehulled: 98.7; Extracted dehulled: 120.2

CHAPTER 11
LEGUME SEEDS

The high nutritive value of the seeds from legume plants has long been recognised, and certain species are important in producing human food. The cost of production, yield per unit area and disease problems like chocolate spot in field beans have traditionally restricted their production as feeding stuffs for animals. In the EEC the production and use of legume seeds as feeds is currently encouraged by the payment of aid. The amount is calculated in relation to the major imported competitors, soya bean meal and, to a lesser extent, maize gluten feed.

Soya bean meal and maize gluten feed are not the only feeds comparable with legumes, and others like the by-products of cotton and palm kernel also compete in the market place. Additional adjustments to the level of aid may be necessary to ensure that peas and beans can be offered on the market competitively. At the time of writing, peas and beans are essentially raw materials for compounders and large-scale farm mixers because only registered processors of animal feeds are able to claim the aid.

Lupins have also been known to man for thousands of years. Seeds of unimproved species are very bitter because of a high content of alkaloids (3%), and until the last 50 years or so they have been used as green manure. For example, they were used during the early years of this century as a pioneer crop on the sandy soils of the Midlands. In recent years, varieties low in alkaloids (0.01 to 0.05 percent in sweet lupin) have been bred.

Sweet lupins are also subject to EEC aid but at present they are little grown in the UK. While they are grown in other parts of Europe, particularly in some Eastern Block countries, they are rarely traded and inclusion in this book is for completeness, and in case the crop becomes more widely available.

| **Feed** | **BEANS (FIELD)** | | *High energy : high protein* |

Description There are many different varieties of bean but the field bean (*Vicia faba* L.) is the one grown for feeding to animals in the UK. The navy bean (*Phaseolus lunatus* L.) is sometimes imported from the US. Varieties of field bean fall into two major groups: Winter and Spring. Both are grown, with winter varieties slightly outyielding spring ones but the latter tending to have higher energy and protein contents.

Physical form Beans are fed cracked, kibbled, coarsely ground or rolled following micronization.

Bulk density 750 to 790 kg/m^3 for whole beans, with values for processed seeds somewhat lower.

DM content 900 g/kg

Typical nutritional specification (gram per kg DM except for energy)

		Winter	Spring		Winter	Spring
	ME (MJ/kg DM)	13.3	13.6	Crude protein	280	340
	D-value	790	810	Oil (method A)	14	13
	NCD	NA	NA	Oil (method B)	NA	NA
	NDF	110	200	Calcium	1	1
	Crude fibre	83	75	Phosphorus	9	5
	Starch	400	360	Magnesium	2	2
	Sugar	NA	NA	Salt	Trace	Trace
	Ash	33	38	Potassium	NA	NA

Nutritional comments Beans are considered primarily as a protein source, but they have a useful energy value which is equal to that of cereals. They are a safe feed for ruminants and their cost-effectiveness and the need for protein in the diet usually determines the level at which they are used. Beans at up to 30% of the diet have been successfully offered to dairy cows. The phosphorus content, particularly in white varieties, is a useful bonus.

Availability More than 300,000 tonnes are grown in the UK.

Relative value index Winter: 125.1; Spring: 133.7

Feed	**PEAS**	*High energy : high protein*

Description
Peas (*Pisum sativa* L.) have been cultivated in temperate regions for many years. Harvested young and tender they are excellent for immediate human consumption or for canning and freezing. For an animal feed peas are usually allowed to become more mature and are harvested using a combine harvester. In recent years their use in animal feeds has increased in the UK and EEC, encouraged by the aid paid to registered processors. This aid is not always sufficient to price them attractively and the aid system is rather complicated to operate.

Physical form
Peas are fed as meal or flaked products. At high levels of inclusion they may present handling problems in the feed mill.

Bulk density
820 to 840 kg/m³

DM content
870 g/kg

Typical nutritional specification (gram per kg DM except for energy)

ME (MJ/kg DM)	13.5	Crude protein	260
D value	890	Oil (method A)	15
NCD	960	Oil (method B)	NA
NDF	132	Calcium	1
Crude fibre	60	Phosphorus	6
Starch	400	Magnesium	2
Sugar	NA	Salt	Trace
Ash	32	Potassium	11

Nutritional comments
The energy and protein contents of peas mean that nutritionally they provide an alternative to soya bean meal and cereal mixtures. The degradability of the protein is classified as B, similar to that of soya bean meal, and the amino acid distribution is similar except that peas are low in methionine. Trypsin inhibitor and phytohaemagglutinins (lectins or toxalbumins) are found in peas, but not in great quantities, particularly in modern varieties. They are destroyed by heat and are not particular problems to ruminants. Peas also contain about 10% tannins, mainly in the seed coat, but again these are less significant to ruminants than to pigs or poultry. Between 10 and 20% may be used in ruminant diets.

Availability
Some peas are usually available, but price-competitiveness depends upon the relative level of aid available.

Relative value index
120.2

Feed	**LUPINS (SWEET)**	*High energy : high protein*

Description

Lupins were known to the Egyptians as early as 2000 BC and there are records of them being described as human food by 400 BC. In more recent years they have been extensively developed in Eastern Europe. There are three commercial types: white flowered (*Lupinus albus* L.), yellow flowered (*L. luteus* L.) and blue flowered (*L. angustifolius* L.). They have occasionally been grown in the UK in the past, primarily as green manure, but recent interest in growing them as a seed crop has not proved successful. The growing season is not long enough and at harvest time the weather is often too damp.

Physical form

Lupins are most easily described as being like small yellow/ brown peas. As with peas they may be milled or flaked for use.

Bulk density

DM content   880 g/kg

Typical nutritional specification (gram per kg DM except for energy)

ME (MJ/kg DM)	13.5	Crude protein	380
D value	NA	Oil (method A)	110
NCD	NA	Oil (method B)	NA
NDF	NA	Calcium	3
Crude fibre	110	Phosphorus	4
Starch	NA	Magnesium	1
Sugar	NA	Salt	2
Ash	40	Potassium	11

Nutritional comments

Historically, the nutritive value of lupin seeds has been limited by their alkaloid content but this is less of a problem in modern selected varieties. Experimentally, levels up to 20% have been included in the diets of dairy cows and beef cattle, successfully replacing a wide range of vegetable proteins. Observations have indicated that their use may result in a slight increase in milk fat production. As with other legume seeds, protein degradability is categorised as B. The protein content of lupins is slightly higher than that of either peas or beans.

Availability

Few lupin seeds are currently available in the UK.

Relative value index   134.2

CHAPTER 12

MARINE AND ANIMAL PROTEINS

Several protein feeds of animal origin are available. Most arise from processing animals or fish for human consumption although certain fishmeals are manufactured from whole fish caught specifically to process for livestock feeds.

Historically, by-products arising from the slaughter, meat processing and rendering industries have been somewhat variable and have been treated with caution and suspicion due to the possibility that they may transmit diseases. Abattoir and port inspections, modern processing procedures and sensitive testing have virtually removed the risk of the spread of disease. Modern plant and process control ensures more reliable and consistent composition of the products.

In modern processing systems for slaughterhouse offal and during rendering different materials can be processed separately, resulting in final products which are consistent at different specifications. For example, meat and bone meals of different qualities (eg protein content) can be produced and marketed as distinctly different products.

Some materials may be processed separately and specifically, to improve their nutritive value. For example, feathers can be hydrolysed to produce feather meal from which the protein is much more readily available than would otherwise be the case.

The composition of fishmeals varies according to whether they arise from offal or from whole fish. They also differ depending upon whether they are from oily fish (herring type) or from white fish.

The type of process by which protein feeds of animal origin are produced has an important influence on their quality. The use of chemicals such as formalin in fish processing, or the type of heating used to dry products can alter the degradability of the protein in the rumen. Flash, ring drying markedly improves the nutritive value of blood meal because it allows the application of sufficient heat to sterilise the product, in addition to drying it. At the same time, this heat does not grossly damage the protein and substantially reduce its overall availability to the animal.

Various protein blends and concentrates may be formulated. These blends can be a highly cost-effective source of protein, particularly when materials, such as blood meal, which alone tend to be unpalatable are blended with others to produce palatable products with a sound nutritional specification. In contrast, when blending is used to incorporate proteins of poor nutritional quality into products, the use of these will result in reduced levels of production and the blends will probably represent poor value for money.

The following tables give information on various fishmeals and by-products from the animal processing industries, together with typical compositional data. However, it should be noted that there may be quite marked variations in nutritional, chemical and physical characteristics between different sources of the same feed and that some sources will exhibit variation between different batches.

Feed	**BLOOD MEAL**	*High energy : high protein*

Description Modern drying methods apply heat gently, which allows blood meal to be produced with a minimum of heat damage. This means that its digestibility is high, even for pigs. Excessive heat substantially reduces its digestibility, although mild heat damage improves the value to ruminants by reducing solubility in the rumen.

Physical form Blood meal is a deep red/brown granular powder. Blood flour is very fine and extremely difficult to handle.

Bulk density

DM content 900 g/kg

Typical nutritional specification (gram per kg DM except for energy)

ME (MJ/kg DM)	13.2	Crude protein	940
D value	860	Oil (method A)	10
NCD	NA	Oil (method B)	NA
NDF	—	Calcium	0.5
Crude fibre	—	Phosphorus	2.5
Starch	NA	Magnesium	0.3
Sugar	NA	Salt	20
Ash	10	Potassium	15

Nutritional comments The dry matter is almost pure protein, which is high in essential amino acids. If appropriately dried the overall availability of the amino acids is high, although their degradation in the rumen is slow and rate of passage of the fine particles is rapid. By itself blood meal appears to be quite unpalatable but blended with other feeds it can be a useful and effective source of protein. Being in a fine form so that its rate of passage is rapid, and having been subjected to heat treatment, protein degradability is considered to be class D. At the time of publishing this book the BSE Order 1988 prevents the use of proteins derived from ruminant tissues being used in diets for ruminants.

Availability Demand for blood meal usually exceeds supply.

Relative value index 195.5

Feed	**FEATHER MEAL (HYDROLYSED)**
	Medium energy : high protein

Description
Raw feathers are insoluble and indigestible because they contain a significant amount of the protein keratin, which contains a high proportion of cystine. When cooked under pressure at an appropriate temperature and for an appropriate length of time the cystine content is reduced and the overall digestibility coefficient is increased to 0.75 or 0.8. The hydrolysed product is dried and ground into a useful source of protein.

Physical form
Hydrolysed feather meal is an off-white or pale brown, friable meal.

Bulk density

DM content
900 g/kg

Typical nutritional specification (gram per kg DM except for energy)

ME (MJ/kg DM)	11.5	Crude protein	890
D value	700	Oil (method A)	50
NCD	NA	Oil (method B)	NA
NDF	—	Calcium	3
Crude fibre	10	Phosphorus	7
Starch	—	Magnesium	2
Sugar	—	Salt	5
Ash	38	Potassium	NA

Nutritional comments
This is a useful source of protein with an energy value below that of blood meal or fishmeal. Insufficient or excessive cooking results in less than optimum protein digestibility. Usually digestibility approaches 0.8, with rumen degradability considered to be class D. Feather meal does not have a high content of the essential limiting amino acids so it is a protein source to be mixed with others, such as blood meal or fishmeal. Ruminant compound feeds may contain up to 10% hydrolysed feather meal provided the overall balance of amino acids is not limiting. It is a useful feed for ruminants while the BSE Order 1988 is effective.

Availability
Some hydrolysed feather meal is usually available throughout the year.

Relative value index
178.0

Feed	**FISHMEAL**	*High energy : high protein*

Description Fishmeals are widely accepted as an excellent protein source but they can vary considerably according to their origin. Traditionally, they were produced from the by-products of processing fish for human consumption and oil extraction. Currently, the demand for fishmeal as an animal feed cannot be met by processing fish offal and trimmings and fish are caught specifically for the purpose. British white (BW) fishmeal is typical of a product from offal, in this case white fish, predominantly cod. Chilean fishmeal is a typical South American (SA) type of fishmeal, manufactured from purpose-caught small fish like Spanish pilchards. In Northern Europe herring type (HT) meals are now often produced from purpose-caught spratt.

Physical form Products are fibrous, sometimes gritty, pale brown or off- white meals.

Bulk density

DM content 900 to 920 g/kg

Typical nutritional specification (gram per kg DM except for energy)

	BW	SA	HT		BW	SA	HT
ME (MJ/kg DM)	14.0	14.5	17.5	Crude protein	720	720	800
D value	720	790	830	Oil (method A)	60	80	95
NCD	NA	NA	NA	Oil (method B)	NA	NA	NA
NDF	—	—	—	Calcium	70	40	25
Crude fibre	—	—	—	Phosphorus	35	25	20
Starch	—	—	—	Magnesium	1.5	2.5	1.5
Sugar	4	NA	4	Salt	20	20	16.5
Ash	220	180	120	Potassium	10	7	12.0

Nutritional comments Fishmeal is a protein feed which combines a biologically good amino acid content with resistance to protein breakdown in the rumen. It is regarded by many as the standard by which other proteins should be judged. Recent trials have both demonstrated the value of fishmeal as a protein source for highly- productive ruminants and shown that its energy value has been substantially underestimated. The degradability of all fishmeals is usually classified as D. While in theory the use of fishmeal should be based on UDP requirements, in practice 5% of the concentrates for high yielding dairy cows and fast growing young beef bulls or lambs seems to be an acceptable rule of thumb. The digestibility/ metabolisability of the protein and oil is relatively constant, although actual contents can be quite variable. The ME value is directly related to protein and oil contents which vary inversely with ash. Taint forming substances in fishmeal are associated with the oil fraction, so where taint may be a problem fishmeal with a low oil content should be selected.

Availability Supplies are usually available all year.

Relative value index British white: 179.5, South American: 183.1, Herring type: 213.5

Feed	**MEAT MEAL**	*High energy : high protein*

Description

Meat meal is a renderer's product manufactured primarily from carcass trim and condensed carcasses. The term *meat meal* is usually reserved for products containing relatively high levels of protein, 60% or more in the DM. To conform with the definition given in Schedule 2 of the Feeding Stuffs Regulations 1988 the product "should be virtually free of hair, bristle, feathers, horn, hoof and skin and of the contents of the stomach and viscera. It shall be technically free of organic solvents." Additionally, legislation requires that "products with a fat content of more than 11% should be described as *rich in fat.*"

Physical form

Meat meal is a brown, slightly fibrous and gritty meal.

Bulk density

DM content

830 g/kg

Typical nutritional specification (gram per kg DM except for energy)

ME (MJ/kg DM)	12	Crude protein	600
D value	65	Oil (method A)	100
NCD	NA	Oil (method B)	NA
NDF	—	Calcium	85
Crude fibre	2	Phosphorus	40
Starch	—	Magnesium	2
Sugar	—	Salt	15
Ash	260	Potassium	NA

Nutritional comments

The nutritional characteristics of meat meals can vary quite considerably. The nature of the material processed influences protein and ash content, whilst the method of treatment affects the amount of oil remaining in the meal. Mechanical extraction results in residues of 10 to 15% oil, whilst solvent extraction reduces the oil to less than 5%. The amount of oil in particular, and to a lesser extent levels of ash affect the ME content. The overall digestibility of the protein is usually above 0.8 and it is assigned to the C category of degradability.

Availability

Meat meal is usually available throughout the year, but at the time of publishing this book the BSE Order 1988 prohibits the use of protein feeds from ruminant animals being fed back to the same or other ruminant species.

Relative value index

155.3

| Feed | **MEAT AND BONE MEAL** | *Medium/high energy : high protein* |

Description

Meat and bone meal differs from meat meal primarily in the amount of bone in the processed material and the protein content of the final product. Meat and bone meal is manufactured mainly from pieces of meat and carcass with a high proportion of bone, but selected to result in a finished product with 40 to 55% protein. Products from different rendering plants have different characteristics and specifications, but the main differences depend upon whether the oil is removed mechanically or by solvent extraction. To conform with Schedule 2 of the Feeding Stuffs Regulations 1988, meat and bone meal "should be substantially free of hair, bristle, feathers, horn, hoof, skin and blood and of contents of the stomach and viscera. It shall be technically free of organic solvents".

Physical form Meat and bone meal is a mid-brown fibrous and gritty meal.

Bulk density NA

DM content 940 g/kg

Typical nutritional specification (gram per kg DM except for energy)

	Mech. extr.	Solv. extr.		Mech. extr.	Solv. extr.
ME (MJ/kg DM)	12.5	11.0	Crude protein	500	550
D value	650	600	Oil (method A)	140	20
NCD	NA	NA	Oil (method B)	NA	NA
NDF	—	—	Calcium	100	115
Crude fibre	15	30	Phosphorus	40	55
Starch	—	—	Magnesium	25	25
Sugar	—	—	Salt	15	20
Ash	300	350	Potassium	NA	NA

Nutritional comments

The nutritional characteristics of meat and bone meal are similar to those of meat meal. The protein content is diluted slightly by an increased level of ash from the increased bone content. The increased ash content is also reflected in slightly higher contents of the major minerals. The protein has a high overall digestibility, with category C degradability. As with all similar products, the amount of residual oil influences composition and particularly the ME content. Energy content is inversely related to ash content.

Availability

Supplies of meat and bone meal are available throughout the year, but at the time of publication of this book the BSE Order 1988 prohibits the use of protein feeds derived from ruminant tissue in the preparation of diets for ruminants.

Relative value index Mechanical: 149.5; Solvent: 143.9

Feed	**POULTRY OFFAL MEAL**	*High energy : high protein*

Description
Poultry offal meal is a composite by-product of poultry processing plants. Heads, feet, emptied intestines, carcass trim, hydrolysed feathers and poultry fat may be included. Composition varies, particularly in relation to the amount of oil which is found in the final product and whether or not feathers are added.

Physical form
Poultry offal meal is a fairly fine, 'fibrous' meal.

Bulk density

DM content
920 g/kg

Typical nutritional specification (gram per kg DM except for energy)

ME (MJ/kg DM)	14.5	Crude protein	650
D value	800	Oil (method A)	150
NCD	NA	Oil (method B)	NA
NDF	—	Calcium	15
Crude fibre	11	Phosphorus	10
Starch	—	Magnesium	2
Sugar	—	Salt	6
Ash	100	Potassium	NA

Nutritional comments
Poultry offal meal can contain up to 250 or even 300 g/kg DM oil, which means that ME contents in excess of 17 MJ/kg DM have been recorded. This may happen when there is a high viscera content. Ash can vary from 60 to 150 g/kg DM, accompanied by considerable variation in Ca and P contents. This meal usually contains moderate levels of lysine and methionine, similar to those found in meat and bone meal. Degradability is usually described as 'low B' or 'high C'. Poultry offal meal is a useful product for ruminants, particularly whilst the BSE Order 1988 remains effective.

Availability
Some meal is usually available most of the year.

Relative value index
177.4

CHAPTER 13

FEEDS FROM MILK PROCESSING

Traditionally the processed or manufactured products from milk are cream, butter and cheese which give rise to the liquid by-products, *skim* or *separated milk, butter milk* and *whey*. Whey can be concentrated by evaporation to crystallise the lactose, leaving another by-product, *delactosed whey*. These traditional by-products range in dry matter content from 50g DM/kg to 400g DM/kg and they are subsequently either dried or distributed as a liquid for inclusion in liquid diets for pigs. Although the traditional processes continue, modern technology such as ultrafiltration or reverse osmosis allows the by-products to be processed further. High quality milk protein can be extracted from skim milk, leaving a lactose-rich liquid which can be treated like whey to produce lactose powder. In time, modern filtration techniques may allow milk products to be dewatered and concentrated much more cheaply than by evaporation.

Skim milk and whey have been given to ruminants in raw and dilute form, but the volumes involved are large and these liquid feeds require specialised facilities compared to conventional forage and concentrate diets. In their raw form they are so dilute that reasonable daily allowances cannot even be offered via a complete diet feeder. Concentrated products, on the other hand, can be transported, distributed and handled more efficiently and can form the basis of highly nutritious liquid feeds.

The nature of milk by-products means that they can be successfully dried only by spray or roller drying, which is costly, and this therefore precludes their use as dry animal feed ingredients except in the manufacture of milk replacers. Surplus whole milk may also be dried, but again the economics of the process are prohibitive if the product is to be used as a livestock feed.

84

| Feed | DELACTOSED WHEY SYRUP | *High energy : high protein* |

Description Whey or mixtures of whey and lactose syrup remaining after protein has been extracted from skim milk are evaporated to about 600 g DM/kg. When cooled the milk sugar, lactose, crystallises out. This is separated by centrifugation and removed for further refining. The delactosed whey syrup remaining is an excellent feed for direct use or to form the basis of a liquid concentrate. It may be handled and fed in bulk and also used in place of molasses to condition feed mixes.

Physical form The syrup is an off-white to pale creamy yellow, sticky, slightly viscous liquid. Delactosed whey is sometimes dried, but it is much more expensive in that form.

Bulk density 1100 kg/m³

DM content 380 g/kg

Typical nutritional specification (gram per kg DM except for energy)

ME (MJ/kg DM)	13.0	Crude protein	250
D value	800	Oil (method A)	—
NCD	NA	Oil (method B)	25
NDF	—	Calcium	40
Crude fibre	—	Phosphorus	30
Starch	—	Magnesium	2
Sugar	460	Salt	66
Ash	200	Potassium	48

Nutritional comments On a dry matter basis delactosed whey differs from whey in that protein and mineral (ash) contents are higher in relation to the residual lactose. The increased ash content means that the ME content per kg DM is reduced. In gross terms delactosed whey is comparable with cereal grain. The protein is of higher biological value and is usually present at a higher concentration, but it can fall when a high proportion of lactose syrup, which contains no protein, is processed through a lactose plant. The main energy source is the residual lactose which, in contrast to sucrose (the main sugar of molasses), has been found in some trials with dairy cows to support the production of high quality milk. The mineral content, which is highly available, is a bonus, although the high NaCl and K contents mean that liberal supplies of drinking water must always be available. Levels of use may be determined by the physical limitations of handling liquids. Inclusion at 5 to 10 kg daily for dairy cows and up to 25% of the dietary DM for beef cattle seems quite acceptable, but in individual situations much higher levels have been used successfully.

Availability Limited quantities of delactosed whey syrup are usually available all year.

Relative value index 50.5

Feed	**WHEY (FRESH)**	*High energy : medium protein*

Description

Whey is the liquid remaining after the removal of coagulated milk solids during the early stages of the manufacture of cheese. Some 80 to 85 litres of whey arise from every 100 litres of whole milk processed. Whey may be dried but the costs of the process prevent the use of dried whey as a general ruminant feed.

Physical form

Whey is a 'thin', off-white liquid with a characteristically milk smell.

Bulk density

1028 kg/m^3

DM content

50 to 70 g/kg

Typical nutritional specification (gram per kg DM except for energy)

ME (MJ/kg DM)	14.0	Crude protein	135
D value	850	Oil (method A)	—
NCD	NA	Oil (method B)	30
NDF	—	Calcium	10
Crude fibre	—	Phosphorus	7
Starch	—	Magnesium	2
Sugar (lactose)	700	Salt	25
Ash	90	Potassium	30

Nutritional comments

Fresh whey, used promptly before it sours, is quite palatable to ruminants. A period of gradual introduction is sometimes necessary and always advisable. The drawback to using whey is its low DM content. Dairy cows have been recorded consuming 100 litres daily and beef cattle up to 45 litres daily at 300 kg liveweight. The nutritive value of the DM is high and both ME and CP contents are higher than cereal grains. All nutrients are highly digestible. The main energy source is the milk sugar, lactose. Its breakdown in the rumen is rapid, which may tend to depress rumen pH, but the use of whey has been associated with increases in milk fat. The protein is also likely to be rapidly degraded (category A), but as it is in suspension, its rate of passage will be rapid and some may escape, undegraded, into the small intestine. In practice, when formulating diets it may be more appropriate to regard degradability as B.

Availability

Supplies are likely to be available most of the year but whey is probably only worth considering if produced locally.

Relative value index

7.6

APPENDIX
PRINCIPAL SOURCES OF REFERENCE

ADAS (1976) *Nutrient Allowances and Composition of Feedingstuffs for Ruminants.* Advisory Paper No 11, 2nd Edition. MAFF, London.

AGRICULTURAL RESEARCH COUNCIL (1976) *The Nutrient Requirements of Farm Livestock Number 4 Composition of British Feedingstuffs.* HMSO, London.

AHERNE, F X and KENNELLY, J J (1983) Oilseed meals for livestock feeding. In: *Recent Advances in Animal Nutrition—1982.* Edited by Haresign, W. Butterworths, London.

BRITISH SOCIETY OF ANIMAL PRODUCTION (1980) *By-products and Waste in Animal Feeding.* BSAP Occasional Publication Number 3. BSAP, Reading.

CENTRAL VEEVOEDER BUREAU IN NEDERLAND (1979) *Veevoedertable.* Lelystad.

COMMISSION OF THE EUROPEAN COMMUNITIES (1985) *Agriculture: Feeding Value of By-products and Their Use by Beef Cattle.* Edited by Boucque, Ch V, Fiems L O and Cottyn B G. C.E.C., Luxembourg.

GÖHL, B (1981) *Tropical Feeds: Feed Information Summaries and Nutritive Values.* FAO Animal Production and Health Series Number 12. FAO, Rome.

GONTZEA, I and SUTZESCU, P (1968) *Natural Antinutritive Substances in Foodstuffs and Forages.* S Karger, Basle.

LONSDALE, C R (1986) Evaluation of by-products. In: *Ruminant Feed Evaluation.* Edited by Stark, B A, Givens, D I and Wilkinson, J M. Chalcombe Publications, Marlow Bottom, Bucks.

MAFF (1986) *Feed Composition: UK Tables of Feed Composition and Nutritive Value for Ruminants.* Chalcombe Publications, Marlow Bottom, Bucks.

MAFF (1988) *Agriculture: The Feeding Stuffs Regulations 1988.* Statutory Instrument 1988 No. 396. HMSO, London.

WAINMAN, F W and DEWEY, P J S (undated) *Feedingstuffs Evaluation Unit. Brief Report Series.* Rowett Research Institute, Aberdeen.

WAINMAN, F W, DEWEY, P J S and BOYNE, A W (1975) *Feedingstuffs Evaluation Unit, First Report 1975.* Rowett Research Institute, Aberdeen.

WAINMAN, F W, DEWEY, P J S and BOYNE, A W (1978) *Feedingstuffs Evaluation Unit, Second Report 1978*. Rowett Research Institute, Aberdeen.

WAINMAN, F W, DEWEY, P J S and BREWER, A C (1984) *Feedingstuffs Evaluation Unit, Fourth Report 1984*. Rowett Research Institute, Aberdeen.

INDEX TO FEEDS